Refugee Number 33,333

Refugee Number 33,333

Farhad Pirbal

translated from the Kurdish by
Pshtiwan Babakr
&
Shook

PHONEME
MEDIA

DEEP
VELLUM

DALLAS, TEXAS

Phoneme Media, an imprint of Deep Vellum Publishing
3000 Commerce St., Dallas, Texas 75226
deepvellum.org · @deepvellum

Deep Vellum is a 501c3 nonprofit literary arts organization founded in 2013 with the mission to bring
the world into conversation through literature.

Text copyright © 1992, 1999, 2004, 2006, 2007, 2009 by Farhad Pirbal
Translation copyright © 2024 by Pshtiwan Babakr and Shook

First edition, 2024
All rights reserved.

Support for this publication has been provided in part by grants from the National Endowment for the
Arts, the Texas Commission on the Arts, the City of Dallas Office of Arts and Culture, the Communities
Foundation of Texas, and the Addy Foundation.

Paperback ISBN: 978-1-64605-271-4 | Ebook ISBN: 978-1-64605-292-9

LIBRARY OF CONGRESS CATALOGING-IN-PUBLICATION DATA

Names: Pirbal, Ferhad, 1961- author. | Babakr, Pshtiwan, translator. |
Shook, David (Poet), translator.
Title: Refugee number 33,333 / Farhad Pirbal ; translated from the Kurdish
by Pshtiwan Babakr & Shook.
Other titles: Penahendey jimare 33 333. English | Refugee number
thirty-three thousand three hundred thirty-three
Description: First US edition. | Dallas, Texas : Phoneme Media/Deep Vellum,
2024.
Identifiers: LCCN 2024008935 (print) | LCCN 2024008936 (ebook) | ISBN
9781646052714 (trade paperback) | ISBN 9781646052929 (ebook)
Subjects: LCGFT: Poetry.
Classification: LCC PK6908.9.P568 P4613 2024 (print) | LCC PK6908.9.P568
(ebook) | DDC 891/.5971--dc23/eng/20240317
LC record available at https://lccn.loc.gov/2024008935
LC ebook record available at https://lccn.loc.gov/2024008936

Cover design by Pablo Marin, Verbum.Media

Interior layout and typesetting by KGT & SHOOK

PRINTED IN UNITED STATES OF AMERICA

Contents

A Poet among Potato Eaters:
An Introduction to Farhad Pirbal

Shook

A man steps directly into oncoming traffic on the road leading into Hewlêr International Airport. The driver of a white truck slams on its brakes, then attempts to skirt the figure, now jerking frantic kicks in his direction, shouting fiercely as he flaps his arms in the air. Farhad Pirbal—his signature mustache bulging like a wilder, unkempt heir to Flaubert—attracts dozens of honks and raised cellphones, documenting the latest of his wide-eyed misadventures for Facebook and YouTube, where they will certainly go viral. That afternoon, they do: the poéte maudit of Kurdistan, taxi matador, cursing his fellow Kurds for their inaction in opposing the Iranian and Turkish bombardment of the mountainous borderlands of Iraqi Kurdistan. Known for the past decade as much for his highly publicized antics as for his prolific literary output, Pirbal, who holds a doctorate in literature from the Sorbonne, is, by his own admission, not well. But in a region with extremely limited mental health resources, the tragedy of his long-term mental malaise has blossomed into full-blown, untreated illness. In a speech he gave in 2013, Pirbal himself indicted his fellow Kurds for their treatment of him: "Even the nomads don't leave behind their madmen, but the Kurds have left me behind." Despite being one of Iraqi Kurdistan's most accomplished poets and prose stylists, his mental illness has led to multiple stints in prison, the country's closest thing to a psychiatric hospital.

Pirbal, born in 1961, may be the greatest innovator of Kurdish literature in the twentieth century, in both poetry and prose. His first collection,

Exil, written between 1984 and 1990 in his hometown of Hewlêr (the capital of the Kurdistan Region of Iraq known in Arabic as Erbil) and in Paris, displays the influence of the French Surrealists and other European schools, an engagement with international literatures that Pirbal argues was essential to the development of early twentieth-century Kurdish literature. A restless

experimentalist, he explores visual poetry in short poems in the shape of the Eiffel Tower and even introduces the calligram, in his depiction of a tree made from the Arabic word for "immortality," which was also the name of a former fiancée:

Pirbal's close relationship with the visual arts seeps into his poetic oeuvre in other ways, too, with occasional incursions of handwritten statements and his invention of the Kurdish erasure poem, redacted with manual flourish, as in his radically counter-nationalist reimagining of the poet Dildar's beloved 1930s anthem "Oh, Foe!" (p. 139), whose ending inverts and truncates the original's militant declaration of Kurdish identity:

**Don't say the Kurds ~~are dead, the Kurds~~ are alive,
~~our flag is alive and bows before none.~~**

His formal innovations extend to his stylized prose work as well. The pages of his 2001 novella *Lieutenant Tahsin and More . . .* , whose concept he first sketched out in Copenhagen in 1987, are split horizontally across their middles, recounting two versions of the titular lieutenant's story, the first set during the day and the second set at night.

Pirbal's earliest work displays a keen sense of nostalgia for simpler times, the Kurdistan of his boyhood recollections, before "the taste of moonlight and spirited songs [had] faded from the tablecloth." Later in that same poem, titled with the address of his childhood home in Hewlêr, he laments, "What bad fortune! My childhood is far away, so far away; my death is even farther." Like his contemporary Abdulla Pashew his poetry is a chronicle of exile and displacement, longing and not belonging. The nine songs of his series "Romantic Songs of Exile" (pp. 143-151) catalog the full range of his experiences during his years in Europe. The casual to-do list that is song five culminates in the question-exclamation of the precariousness that undergirds the exile's every action, while song six asks a series of twenty questions about where the disoriented poet might presently find himself in Europe before a final question that reveals a wistful longing for the familiarity and beauty of his homeland, seen through his "smiling windows":

(5)

Hem my pants
Button
Precipitation stops, meaning the weather is getting better
Call Hawre to get Hiwa's address
Vestaport's dense, empty forest
Rip up the letters, or burn them: and only keep my mother's
Shoes, shoemakers, keys
Lars's debts. Sell the refrigerator to Maria
All my IDs and documents
The train to Norway departs at eleven thirty at night

A letter to Aras in Munich
To Aram in Amsterdam
To Taha in Canada
And a letter to ol' Bachtyar in Sablagh, telling him:
"I will leave here for good in a few days:
I still don't know where to?!"

(6)

[...] Am I still in that cold black swamp in Europe
or in the high-up, quiet
room
with my two beautiful,
smiling windows,
in the neighborhood of Tairawa in Hewlêr?

By song seven, the poet engages in wistful bargaining, contrasting the supposed luxuries of France with a simple beauty of a childhood tree. The entire series reaches its climax in a single couplet that reminds us—with the same sly grin Pirbal often flashes in real life—that a return to one's homeland is not a return from exile, because there is no return from exile:

(7)

Your streets, oh Europe,
your gardens,
your leaders,
your museums,
your police men, young girls, women, windows, doors,
squares, cats, chimneys, boats, trains,
cars, fountains, airports, telephone booths,
banks, police stations, restaurants,

sea shores, rooftops,
your dogs,
your passports
all of your things, oh Europe,
I sacrifice them all for *the tree in our front yard.*

(9)

I returned to Hewlêr: to find my childhood.
I bumped into my youth: it was getting old.

In much of Pirbal's post-European work, his poet/narrator traverses that unknown distance toward death, a stranger wandering an unfamiliar homeland, not unlike the wandering mystics of an earlier Kurdistan. He ends a poem from 1991 with a confused question that now seems to foresee his life's own quandaries, posed equally to society and to poetry itself:

I walked with poetry;
poetry, like me, meandered
meanderer:
it didn't know where we should head?

•

While his early poems already displayed a characteristic compassion, by the mid-1990s he began to more directly advocate for social justice, as in his poem "1993" (p. 95):

As long as the price of a shoe in Paris
is enough to feed 30 of the hungry in Siberia,
as long as 3 cold Swedish krona
is worth 33 days in the lives of 33 of the hungry in Somalia,

as long as the price of a Pepsi-Cola in Chicago
is worth the monthly salary of an employee
gone unpaid in Hewlêr, [...]
this world must be destroyed—entirely!

This insistence in the destruction of unfairness and inequality, an equally strong disdain of societal impositions on individual freedoms, and Pirbal's willingness to so directly and so publicly speak his mind have invited trouble in Iraqi Kurdistan's tense political arena.

Pirbal has also chosen to largely ignore regional political affiliations. After returning from Paris at the outset of the Iraqi Kurdish Civil War, doctorate in hand, he began a teaching career at Salahaddin University, where he maintained relationships with writers and publishers on both sides of Kurdistan's primary political divide. Unusually for a writer from Hewlêr, whose populace is typically affiliated with the Kurdistan Democratic Party (KDP), many of his books were published in Slemani, three hours east toward the Iranian border, whose citizens are typically affiliated with the Patriotic Union of Kurdistan (PUK). Even after the newfound freedoms Kurdish literature and language enjoyed after emerging from the civil war, his groundbreaking novella *Lieutenant Tahsin and More...* proved too much for the PUK-affiliated Central Peshmerga Leadership Command, which joined the Kurdish Women's Union to file a lawsuit against the author, accusing the work of disrespecting culturally hallowed peshmerga forces and women. Over seventy articles about the book appeared that week, and booksellers in every bazaar in Kurdistan hawked pirated editions of the sold-out novella at tenfold its original price. By then, Pirbal was so respected a figure that late party leader and beloved patriarch Jalal Talabani intervened, requesting the withdrawal of the lawsuit and even penning an editorial for *Kurdistani News* advocating for Pirbal's freedom of speech.

More recently, Pirbal's relationship to the political powers that be has primarily resulted in his persecution. His active social media presence has grown into a significant platform for disseminating his views, with over 250,000 combined Facebook likes and follows. His airport outburst took place in

2013, and he was arrested soon thereafter. The Hewlêri Police Department still catalogs the video of the incident on their official YouTube account. In 2016, Pirbal was arrested again, in his underwear, for attempting to urinate on the Appellate Court of Hewlêr, protesting the cronyism of both the dominant rival political parties. For many Kurds, his indictment rang true: "If you aren't a whore or a bastard, they won't give you a job opportunity. That's why I raise my head. I piss on this government!" The following April, Pirbal was attacked by two young men, in what was widely presumed to be political retaliation. In 2018, the public prosecutor for Hewlêr requested the writer's arrest, alleging he had received several complaints from the public about his behavior. Soon thereafter, Pirbal's brother revealed that he had requested his sibling's stay in prison, for his own protection, and asked the government, political parties, and public to protect Pirbal from politics. "He is sick and needs to be cured."

●

In the predawn hours of July 14, 2019, Pirbal broke into the bookstore and offices of the Wafayi publishing house, which had recently announced that they would be publishing new editions of his complete works, in standalone volumes beginning with his seminal short story collection *The Potato Eaters* and his study of world literature *The Literary Movements*. Lit only by the glow of his cigarette and cellphone, he moved through the space, dousing books and desks with gasoline. On his way out, he flicked the cigarette's cherry from its filter. The gasoline caught, and the bookstore burned to the ground. That morning, the poet freely admitted to the crime, which he claimed was just retribution for the publisher's failure to pay him as agreed. In a public letter of apology, his brother attributed the behavior to addiction to unspecified drugs. After two months in prison, Pirbal was released on bail after making an initial payment toward the damages owed to his former publisher. Today he continues to live in Hewlêr, alone in a home cluttered with books and overflowing with his paintings, often made directly on the dwelling's walls, and sculptures made of found objects. Though his work is widely known in

Kurdistan, where his celebrity is such that he is recognized on the street, this volume, along with his short story collection *The Potato Eaters* (Deep Vellum, 2024), translated by Jiyar Homer and Alana Marie Levinson-LaBrosse, comprise the first significant selections of his work in English.

The title story from *The Potato Eaters*, one of the best-known short stories of contemporary Kurdish literature, features a protagonist named Fereydun, who returns from thirteen years abroad to find his home village has been forced by famine to eat solely potatoes, which they have learned to prepare according to infinite techniques, even producing potato wine. Eventually, they quit wanting to eat anything else. The community learns to make clothes from potato peels, and they hang portraits of their favorite potatoes on the walls of their homes. So great is their appreciation for the tuber that even "When someone died, they washed the body with potato water and, in the end, laid a single potato, to rest in the grave." Received as a great writer, Fereydun is wined and dined for four days. After consuming the countless potatoes placed before him, he is finally able to reveal the contents of the bulging bag that he has carried with him on his long journey home. With a proud grin, Fereydun empties his sack of its host of gold coins, nuggets, and bricks. Confused, his father asks, "So, you didn't bring any potatoes from abroad?" Each family member repeats the question in turn, as Fereydun grows more exasperated, until he's not sure if it is he or his family that has gone mad. Finally his father, clearly ashamed of his son, asks, "Well, son, but what is gold? What is it good for?"

In a world where everyone prizes potatoes, Fereydun's riches are a confounding embarrassment. Today, Pirbal's are no less confounding. Like his character, he traveled the world, saving what gold he could to bring home. But Pirbal has no narrator to help us recognize him for the hero, for the sane man in a world gone mad.

Translators' Note

"There is not expleanation every time for every thing"
—Farhad Pirbal, "Blue Rainbow"

The above epigraph, which appears, inexplicably in English with its extra e, in Pirbal's 1999 poem "Blue Rainbow," must console us as translators, as translating this volume has been the most challenging endeavor of our careers. Fortunately the challenge has corresponded to the joy in undertaking the task, which has been accompanied by a soundtrack of laughter, equally at our own mistakes and at Pirbal's dark humor. While Pirbal has been generous to us when we've approached him, stumped by his language or by his encyclopedic references, he himself has not always known the answer to our questions. At times he has forgotten where he was when he composed a poem, or may not have known his precise location at the time he composed it, or may have only heard its name through the scrim of various other languages. At other times he has invented geographies and histories, the imagination his truest homeland. The fallibility of memory is central to Pirbal's work, and more often than not the precise locations where his exile took place are secondary to his experiences and emotions. We have endeavored to keep that in mind as translators, that we may echo the essential Pirbalian spirit that breathes in and through these poems.

To prioritize the reader's initial experience of the poems, we have compiled substantial endnotes to this volume, so that those interested may learn more about the many known Kurds, Iraqis, and others Pirbal references throughout, as well as some of the history and politics that serve as a backdrop to his poetry. We have included a significant selection of Pirbal's visual poems, alongside English-language keys. Because Kurdish reads from right to left and because its syntax is often considerably more flexible regarding word order than English, we have sometimes reordered the words in our keys for ease of reading comprehension. Because of how unique these visual poems are in Kurdish poetry—indeed, Pirbal is the only Kurdish poet we know of to have experimented with concrete poetry or erasure poems—we have sought to include as many as possible, even when the image quality of the Kurdish-language originals appears degraded, as in the original Kurdish publications.

A restless innovator and experimentalist, Pirbal employs punctuation and line breaks according to a shifting grammar decidedly his own. Despite an initial impulse toward manuscript-wide standardization, we have for the most part sought to retain Pirbal's idiosyncratic use of semicolons, parentheses, and other marks, in the belief that the occasional ambiguity encountered by the English-language reader will parallel that of the Kurdish. That said, we have in some instances added marks to alleviate potential grammatical confusion in English, and we have often translated the poet's punctuation, seeking to replicate the effect of the punctuation employed on a poem-by-poem basis, rather than simply reproducing identical marks, which are often used distinctly in Kurdish. Given the chronological assembly of this volume of selected poems, it is our hope that the reader will also notice how Pirbal's use of punctuation and line breaks evolves over time, alongside his subject matter.

There are also several instances in this manuscript where we have sought to retain the Kurdish flavor of the language at the expense of the idiomatic. This manifests in two primary instances: the first, when Kurdish employs the language of the body; the latter, in various forms of poetic reduplication. One example of the former is our translation of "the city's liver" (جەرگەی شار), in "Nasir 'Shaida' Mohammed." The phrase is the Kurdish equivalent of "downtown," which we had initially used. Upon revision, its poetry made it an obvious choice for our translation, though it sounds stranger and more elaborate in English than the original does to the Kurdish ear. Fellow Pirbal translator Alana Marie Levinson-LaBrosse has eloquently written about this phenomonon as it manifests in the work of both contemporary and classical Kurdish poetry. The second instance consists of the multiple forms of playful reduplication employed in Sorani, and particularly in its poetry, at both the level of the syllable and the word. We have often chosen to retain the repetition in English when inflective, that is, when dealing with nouns and adverbs that are repeated to denote plurality, added intensity, or repetition ("slowly-slowly" and "oppressor oppressor," for example). In instances of lexical derivation, we have prioritized intelligibility in English—one example is the phrase we've rendered "feqês and whatnot," toward the end of *I Remember . . .* , in which instance Pirbal appends a rhyme in Kurdish to make "feqê and meqê" (فه‌قێ و مه‌قێ), suggesting something akin to "whatnot." (Thanks to our copyeditor Shene Mohammed for her suggestion!) *I Remember...* also features a number of political and protest slogans, as well as nursery rhymes. In our translation we have prioritized rhyme and musicality, in an effort to stay true to the spirit of the genre, and in our endnotes we have provided word-for-word translations and any additional context necessary.

Like most migrants and almost all Kurds, Pirbal is multilingual by necessity, and this polyglotism is reflected in his poetry. These poems contain significant Arabic, which reflects the reality of daily life in the Kurdistan Region of Iraq. (Pirbal has written poetry entirely in Arabic, but we have not included that work here.) The book also includes bits of English, French, Italian, and Turkmen, sometimes written in the Sorani orthography, often with a Pirbalian accent or affectation. Pirbal alludes to literature written in even more languages. In general, we have opted to use Kurdish place names and name spellings, unless Pirbal intentionally chose otherwise (as in his use of the historical name Arbela in reference to Hewlêr in "Border"). Pshtiwan also encountered notable dialectical variation between the Sorani spoken in Hewlêr, where Pirbal is from, and Slemani, where he is from. With Shene Mohammed's assistance, we have used the Library of Congress' system for latinizing Sorani, though we have made considerable exceptions when alternate spellings are well known or might allow the reader to more easily locate additional information about people, places, or events. While there are several systems for the latinization of Sorani, little standardization exists in practice.

We began collaborating on this translation in the fall of 2018, just weeks after Shook arrived in Slemani, at Kashkul, the center for arts and culture at the American University of Iraq, Sulaimani, where Pshtiwan was a Principal Investigator and they were the new Artist in Residence. In fact, the first book in Kurdish Shook ever owned was the edition of Pirbal's selected poems that most of this volume's contents come from, gifted and inscribed by Pshtiwan, who wrote, "Hope to see this book in English." Over the course of two years together in Kurdistan, we worked intermittently on the translation. In the spring of 2021, we reunited in Iowa City, where, over the course of five weeks, we generated the bulk of the present manuscript, which we then polished over the next two years.

Pshtiwan was drawn to translating Farhad Pirbal's poetry because of his ability to capture the experience of exile and the sense of displacement felt by many Kurds. During and soon after his undergraduate years, Pirbal's *Literary Movements* was a key reference for Pshtiwan and his social circle of emerging artists and intellectuals, and he was part of a theater group who put on one of Pirbal's plays. When he began this translation journey, he had never personally experienced living outside of his home city. However, two years into the project, he found himself carrying his home on his shoulders as he moved from one place to another. Pirbal's own journey is one of displacement and separation from his beloved Hewlêr, leading him through Iran, Denmark, Poland, and France before he returned to Kurdistan in 1994. In parallel, Pshtiwan left his hometown Slemani in late 2019, and moved to the United States. After a series of relocations from one state to another, he ultimately returned to Kurdistan in 2023, this time to Hewlêr, where Pirbal himself today resides.

In spring 2023, with Phoneme/Deep Vellum as our publisher, we discovered two collections of Pirbal's poetry previously unknown to us, a result of Kurdistan's fractured publishing system and book market. We quickly added representative selections from *The Book of Dreams* and *27 Pieces of Bone*, so that this initial volume of Pirbal's work in English could be as representative as possible. The selection of the poems in this volume was primarily Pshtiwan's responsibility, although Shook did contribute to that discussion, based partly on the knowledge of Pirbal's poetry they gained through their work cotranslating an overlapping but distinct selection of his poetry into Spanish with Jiyar Homer. It is our hope that much more of Pirbal's work someday find a receptive readership in English, alongside this volume and his simultaneously published short story collection *The Potato Eaters*, cotranslated by Jiyar Homer and Alana Marie Levinson-LaBrosse.

Shook
Newt Beach, CA

Pshtiwan Babakr
Hewlêr, Kurdistan

October 2023

Exil
١٩٩٠

Exil
1990

ڕۆحی پەژموردە

بە زایە چوو لە ملایەعنییا هەموو وەقتم، یەعنی
دەبێ وەقتێ لە بولوەقتێ بخوازمەوە تا تیا بمرم
مەحوی

هەر پارچەیەکی بوونم، ژیانم
لە دەمەوخۆر ئاوابوونێک
لە دورگەیەک
لە پەنا دارێک
لە پاڵ ئازارێک
لێ
بە
جێ
ما:
چاوم لە تاران، خەیاڵاتم لە ئەنقەرە
پارەوپوولم لە دیمەشق، دڵم لە وارشۆ
گوڕی خوێنیشم، لە بەندەرە سڕەکانی کۆپنهاگن

لە شەقامە ساردەکانی نیوەشەوان
سەرگەردان
بێ چەتر
لە ژێر باراندا
وەک گەڵایەکی زەردی وەریوی دەم با
دەخوولێمەوە:
عەودالْی
ژوورێکم
بە ئەندازەی
هۆنراوێک
کە ڕۆحی خۆمی تیا حەشار بدەم.

Withered Soul

All my hours were vainly spent—even to die
I must beg the Lord of Time for more.
                              —Mahwi

each piece of my being, my life
at sunset
on an island
in the shelter of a tree
beside a wound
I
left
it:
my eyes in Tehran, my imagination in Ankara
my cash and change in Damascus, my heart in Warsaw
the racing of my blood, in the numb harbors of Copenhagen

on the cold, midnight streets
vagrant
no umbrella
beneath the rain
like a fallen yellow leaf in the wind
I whirl:
I yearn for
a room
the size of
a poem
where I can hide my soul.

حەوت ساڵەیی

حەیاتێکی ترم دی: خزم و خوێشان دەورەیان دابووم
سەر لە نوێ هاتمەوە دنیا بە ڕۆح وەک تۆڵفی ساوا بووم
پیرەمێرد

حەوت ساڵان بووم
حەزم دەکرد بۆ پەپوولەیەک، کەروێشکێک، گوڵێک، بنووشتێمەوە؛ بدوێم

حەوت ساڵان بووم
حەزم دەکرد باوەشێک وەکوو باوەشی خوشک ڕۆحی کەسیرەم ئامێز
بگرێ.

حەوت ساڵان بووم
خەونێکی بچووک، ئەگەرچی ساکار، نیوەشەو خەوی لێ دەزڕاندم.
شتێکی بچووک، ئەگەرچی ساکار، تا خەم حەز بکا هۆن هۆن دەیگریاندم.

ساڵێک
دوو ساڵ
دە ساڵ
پازدە ساڵ
بیست ساڵ بەسەر حەوت ساڵیمدا ڕابورد:
گەلێک شاری تازە گەڕام
ئەزموونێکی یەکجار زۆرم کۆکردەوە
قژم تاڵ تاڵ
سپی هەڵگەڕا
کەچی نەمتوانی-
نەمتوانی تۆزقاڵێک چییە
گەورە ببم.

Being Seven

I saw another life, surrounded by kin
I returned to the world with a newborn's soul.
—Piramerd

I was seven
I liked to bow before a butterfly, a rabbit, a flower; to talk

I was seven
I liked a hug, like my sister's, arms around my weary soul

I was seven
a small dream, simple as it might be, would keep me awake in the middle of
the night
a small thing, simple as it might be, would make me cry softly for as long as
sorrow delighted in it

a year
two years
ten years
fifteen years
twenty years passed those seven by:
I traveled to many new cities
gathered so many experiences
strand by strand
my hair turned white
yet I could not
I could not—
to even the slightest degree
grow up

تەیراوە
خانووی ژمارەی ٢٩٧

شامی هەموو نەهار و فوسوولی هەموو بەهار
تۆزی هەموو عەبیر و، بوخاری هەموو بوخوور
نالی

من هەمیشە بیر لە خانوویەک دەکەمەوە
بیر لە ڕێیەک، لە شوێن پێیەک؛ بمباتەوە سەر ئەو خانووە.

لەوەتەی سفرە تامی تریفە و گۆرانی سۆزی ون کردووە، من هەر دەگەڕێم
و دەگەڕێم.
لەوەتەی ژوورەکەم بۆنی ڕۆتین و ژێر هەنگڵی عارەقاوی سۆزانییەکانی
گرتووە.

من هەر دەپرسم و دەپرسم.
لە هەموو سمۆرەیەکم پرسیوە، لە هەموو پۆلە واژەیەکی بەناوسالکەوتووی
کە لە هەوارە ڕەنگینەکانی مندالّی و عەشق و گوڵمەزەکان دەگەڕێنەوە.

ئەو خانووە با لە یەکجار دوورەوەش بێ، دەیناسمەوە:
دیوارەکانی   بە هەستی هەورینی میهرەبانی هەڵچنراون؛
پەنجەرەکەی   بە پێشبینییەکی لاکێشەیی تریفەدار؛
گڵۆپەکانی   زەردەخەنەی مندالیمان تێدا دەسووتێ.

ئەو خانووە، هەیوانەکەی جێژوانی تێک ئالّانی هەست و گیایە،
پەیژەیەکی بچکۆلەی لێیە   کە عیشق و هەوەس پێیدا بەرەو
سەربانی سەوزی کامڵبوون و خەونبینین سەردەکەون.
ئەو خانووە جوێباریکی بەخشندەری پێیدا تێدەپەڕێ:
هەر وەرزەی ڕەنگێک، هەر ڕۆژەی دەنگێک، هەر ساتەشی تامێکی هەیە.

مخابن! مندالّیم دوورە؛ تا بڵێی دوور؛ مردنیشم لە ئەو دوورتر.

Tairawa

House Number 297

Its evenings all mornings, its seasons all spring,
Its dust all rosewater, its steam all incense
—Nali

I always think of a house
think of a pathway, of footprints, which lead me back to that house.

Since the taste of moonlight and passionate songs have faded from the
    tablecloth, I have wandered and wandered.
Since my room has taken on the scent of routine and the sweaty armpits of
    prostitutes.

I ask and ask.
I have asked every squirrel, every aged eagle
returning from the colorful huts of childhood, love, and mischief.

Even when distant, I remember that house:
its walls   are built with the cloudy feelings of kindness;
its window   a rectangular, moonlit prediction;
its lamps   burning with our childhood laughter.

That house, its terrace is emotions on a date with the grass, embracing.
There is a small ladder,   which love and lust
climb to the green roof of growing up and dreaming.
That house, a merciful stream passing through it
with a color for each season, a sound for each day, and a taste for each
    moment.
What bad fortune! My childhood is far away, so far away; my death is even
    further.

هەنگاو. هەنگاو...

هەر ئاواتێک بۆنی گیا و گوێزی لێ بێ، بەرەو ڕووی دەچم.
هەر تراویلکەیەک لە دەرەوشانەوەی ئاسوودەی خۆیدا بانگم بکا، بەرەو
ڕووی دەچم.

چ ڕێگایەکی سەخت و دژوارە؛
ڕەشەبایەکی توندە دەنگی دێ!
بەڵام من بەم گەڕانە بێهوودەیەی خۆم ڕاهاتووم.

لە خۆم بێکەسێ، لە خۆم غەریبێ:
زۆر دەترسم لەم ئاواییە نامۆیەدا گۆڕغەریب بم!

ئاه!
لە ئێوارەیەکی وێرانکراوی وردوخاشدا بوو کە ماڵئاواییم لەو خانووە کرد:
هەنگاوەکانم ئاوڕیان لە دەرگا هەورینەکەی دەدایەوە و
هۆن — هۆن دەگریان.

Step by step . . .

Any of my desires that smell of grass and walnuts, I approach.
Any mirage that calls me with its glimmering comfort, I approach.

What a rocky and arduous path—
the sound of a strong wind!
But I am used to this absurd searching.

What a lonely man I am, what a stranger:
scared to be buried a stranger in this strange village!

Oh!
It was on a devastated evening, crushed into pieces, that I bade that house
    farewell:
my footsteps stared back at its cloudy door
and they cried.

تاسه

پ	پ
ر	ر
ج	ت
م	

ج	ج
ا	ا
و	و
م	ت

پ	پ
ه	ه
ن	ن
ج	ج
م	ت

هێندەیئەهریمەنیمردنحەزبكاتاسەوغەریبییەكتردەكەن

Longing

Y	M
R	Y
H	H
A	A
I	I
R	R
Y	M
R	Y
E	E
Y	Y
E	E
S	S
Y	M
R	Y
F	F
I	I
N	N
G	G
E	E
R	R
S	S

longforeachotherasmuchasdeathlyahrimanwants

ناسر محەمەد شەیدا

ناوی ناسر بوو
خەڵکی درەختە سووتاوەکانی دامێن شاخێک بوو
نرکە و ناڵەی ئاویلکەدانی شەقامەکان بانگیان کردە شار: ناوجەرگەی شار.

ماڵەکەیان، – من خۆم دیبووم– لە تاقە چرایەک زیاتر، هیچی دیکەی تێدا
نەبوو:
چرای دڵی، چاوی ناسر.

ناسر، شەیدای کردبوو بە نازناوی خۆی.

ئەو ماوەیە، ئێمە هەموومان حەزمان دەکرد نازناومان هەبێ:
پەرۆش، پەریشان، خامۆش، غەمبار
ئەویش "شەیدا" شەیدای وڵات، شەیدای ئازادی.

ناسر، ئەوکات
سەرۆک شانەی کۆمیتەی ناوشار بوو.

ناسر، پڕ قورگی: ئێوارەی برسی و حەژمەتاویی کرێکاران بوو
تریفەی دەردی بێ وڵاتی بە سیمایەوە، دەتگوت نووری شکۆمەندی
مووغەکانە.

ناسر هەر لە پیکابی گوند گەیشتنان تا خۆر کەوتنان
تیشکی بەخشندەی تریفەی واژە تازەکانی
بەسەر کارگە و گەڕەکە برسی، تاریکەکاندا دابەش دەکرد.
ئەو دەیەویست هەر کوکوختییەک کاژێکی هەبێ.

ناسر پردێک بوو لە نێوان پەنجەرە و کۆڵان،
بێدەنگی و هاوار،
کۆیلایەتی و ڕاچڵەکینی ڕۆح.
ناسر لە ۱۹۸۱/۷/۱۶ گیرا:
باران لە تەری چۆوە، کلپە لە ئاگر چۆوە، گەڵا لە سەوزی چۆوە؛

Nasir "Shaida" Mohammed

His name was Nasir.
He came from the torched trees at the foot of a mountain.
The moans and groans of dying streets called him to the city: the city's liver.

Their house—I had seen it myself—besides a single lantern, there was
    nothing:
the lantern of Nasir's heart, Nasir's eyes.

Nasir took Shaida, "eager," as his nickname.

At that time, we all loved having nicknames:
Parosh, "heartsick," Pareshan, "distressed," Xamosh, "quiet," Ghambar, "sad."
He chose Shaida, eager for country, eager for freedom.

Nasir, back then,
was the city committee unit leader.

Nasir, his throat full of a worker's sad, hungry evenings—
on his face, the moon of homelessness' ache, as if the glorious light of a bull.

Nasir, from the arrival of the village pickups till sunset,
distributed the generous moonlight of new words
over the dark and hungry factories and neighborhoods.
He wanted each dove to have its own pine.

Nasir was a bridge between the window and the alley outside,
between silence and scream,
between slavery and the soul's awakening.
Nasir was arrested on 7/16/1981:
the rain lost its wetness, the fire its flame, the color green its leaves,

چایخانەکان، شەقامەکان، نامیلکە و بەیانە نهێنییەکان پرسەیان بۆ داگرت.
شەهامەتی، هۆن هۆن فرمێسکی بۆ هەڵدەڕشت.

لە مفاوەزاتی ساڵی هەشتا و چوار
گوتیان: "ناسر ئازاد دەکرێ."
گوتیان: "رۆژنامە ئازاد دەکرێ."
گوتیان: "تەلەفزیۆن ئازاد دەکرێ."
گوتیان: "جوتیار، باڵندە، باران، گیا قوتابی، هەور، خۆشەویستی... ئازاد
دەکرێن؛"
بەڵام نە ئەوان، نە ناسریش ئازاد نەکران.

ناسر، نادیار، تاکو ئێستا بێ سەروشوێن:
تەڕیی باران لە بیری کرد.
سەوزیی گەڵا لە بیری کرد.
شەونم، بەهار، کۆڵانەکان، گفتوگۆکان... لە بیریان کرد.

لەوانەیە ئێستا تەنێ من–
تەنێ من بزانم ڕۆژێ لە ڕۆژان
شەڕەلاوێکی قۆڵا هەبوو لە هەولێر
لە گەڕەکی تەیراوە دەژیا...
ناوی ناسر بوو.

کۆپنهاگن ١٩٨٧

chaixanas, streets, leaflets, and secret documents arranged his funeral.
His nobility gently wept.

In the negotiations of '84
they said: "Nasir will be freed."
They said: "The newspapers will be freed."
They said: "The TV channels will be freed."
They said: "The farmworkers, birds, rain, grass, students, clouds, love . . . will
    be freed."
But neither they nor Nasir were freed.

Nasir, invisible, still without a trace:
the rain's wetness forgot him.
The leaves' greenness forgot him.
The dew, spring, alleys, conversations . . . forgot him.

Now, I may be the only one—
the only one who knows that once upon a time
there was a handsome, fit young man in Hewlêr
who lived in the neighborhood of Tairawa . . .
and his name was Nasir.

Copenhagen 1987

Hotel Paradis

لەم سەرزەمینە پانوپۆڕەدا
لە شارێکی فەرامۆش کراوی قەراغ ئاوارەییدا
لە ئوتێلێکی دەرەجە نۆ
لە ژوورێک
لە قوژبنێکی کەسیرەدا
بێ ئاگردان
تەنیا:
دانیشتووم بە دیار
چەند رەسمێکی یازده سال پێش ئەمڕۆوه

د
ە
گ
ر
ی
م
.

.

.

.

Hotel Paradis

on this broad earth

in a neglected city on displacement's shore

in a ninth-degree hotel

in a room

in a cold corner

no fireplace

alone:

I sit with

pictures from eleven years ago

I

w

e

e

p

.

.

.

.

وان ژی هەر نیشتیمانی خۆمانە

برای شیرینم، خەسرۆ گیان
لە نامەکەتدا نووسیوتە، دەڵێی:
"نەمدەتوانی چیتر لە کەرکووک بمێنمەوە
کارکردنم قەدەغە بوو، نانخواردنم قەدەغەبوو، مانەوەم لە ماڵ قەدەغە بوو
پیاسەم، هەناسەم، هەموو شتێکم قەدەغە بوو."
-کەچی خۆ کەرکووک نیشتیمانی خۆشمانە،
برای شیرینم
خۆ کەرکووک نیشتیمانی خۆمانە!

لە نامەکەتدا نووسیوتە، دەڵێی:
"سەری خۆم هەڵگرت، خۆم لەسەر سنووری ئێران دۆزیەوە
حەزم دەکرد بچمە مەهاباد
خوشکە ئاوارە و منداڵەکانی بێنمەوە
بەڵام سەرسنوور، بە مووس، بە ژەهر
بە تاریکایی سەد هەزار پۆلیس تەلبەند کرابوو."
-کەچی خۆ مەهاباد نیشتیمانی خۆشمانە، برای شیرینم
خۆ مەهاباد نیشتیمانی خۆشمانە!

لە نامەکەتدا نووسیوتە، دەڵێی؛
"لەسەر سنووری ئێران، پۆلیس ڕاویان ناین
کە گەیشتمە نزیک هەکاری
بە تەنیا نەبووم: دوو هەزار و پێنج سەد کورد بووین
ئەمجارەیان پۆلیسی تورک داوای پەساپۆرتیان لێ کردین؛
پەساپۆرتی چی؟!
ڕایانپێچاینە هۆتێلێکی گەورەی شاری وان."

لە نامەکەتدا نووسیوتە، دەڵێی:
"ئێستا نۆ رۆژە وام لە شاری وان

Wan Too Is Our Homeland

My sweet brother, dear Khasro,
in your letter you wrote,
"I couldn't stay in Kirkuk any longer:
working was forbidden, eating was forbidden, even staying at home was
    forbidden.
Walking, breathing, everything was forbidden."
        —But Kirkuk is still our homeland,
        my sweet brother,
        Kirkuk is still our homeland!

In your letter you wrote,
"I headed out. I found myself at the border with Iran.
I wanted to go to Mahabad.
To bring back my displaced sister and her children.
But the border was barred with razors, with poison,
with the darkness of one hundred thousand police officers."
        —But Mahabad is still our homeland, my sweet brother,
        Mahabad is still our homeland!

In your letter you wrote,
"At the border of Iran, the police chased us
when I had almost reached Hakari.
I was not alone: there were two thousand five hundred of us Kurds.
This time the Turkish police asked for our passports.
What passports?!
They packed us all into a big hotel in the city of Wan."

In your letter you wrote,
"I have been in the city of Wan for nine days now.

پۆلیسی تورک ڕێمان نادەنێ بچین هەوای پاک و سازگاری ناو شارەکە
هەڵبمژین.
گشت ئێوارەیەک بە بێجامەیەکی خەتخەتەوە
لە پەنجەرەوە تەماشا دەکەم:
وان ناوشارەکەی تا بڵێی خۆشە
شاخەکانی زۆر گەردەنکەش، باخچەکانی گەلێک ڕەنگین
کچەکانیشی: کەزی شۆڕ و
بەژن شۆڕ و
گەلێک نیانن."

نووسیوتە، دەڵێی:
"لەم هوتێلە من تەنیا نیم پەناهەندە
دوو هەزار و پێنج سەد کەسین
پۆلیسی تورک ڕێمان نادەنێ بچین هەوای پاک و سازگاری ناوە شارەکە
هەڵبمژین."
-ئاخر وانیش هەر نیشتیمانی خۆمانە،
برای شیرینم؛
وانیش هەر
نیشتیمانی خۆمانە.

The Turkish police don't let us go outside to breathe the city's fresh air.
Every evening in my striped pajamas
I stare out my window:
downtown Wan is as beautiful as you can possibly describe.
Its mountains, very proud, its gardens, very colorful.
And its girls: long haired and
    tall and
    very gentle."

You wrote,
"I am not the only refugee in this hotel.
There are two thousand five hundred of us.
The Turkish police don't let us go outside to breathe the city's fresh air."
      —But Wan too is still our homeland,
      my sweet brother,
      Wan too
      is our homeland.

چاوەڕێت کردایە، سەروەر!

چاوەڕێت کردایە، سەروەر!
چاوەڕێت کردایە،
ئاخۆ لە نێوان لێوی لەزمی تۆ و لێوی بەیان دا چی سەوز دەبوو!

چاوەڕێت کردایە: ئاخۆ لە شوێنی ئەو کەڵاوانەی
کە ئێوارە ژەنگگرتووەکان لاشەی بۆگەنبووی برینەکانمان تێدا دەناشتن
چی سەوز دەبوو؟

چاوەڕێت کردایە:
ئاخۆ لەسەر ئەو تاشە بەردە قەوزەییانەی
کە شەوانی ئێشکگرتن سەری ماندوومان پێدا دەگرتن
چی سەوز دەبوو؟

چاوەڕێت کردایە
ئەی براترین و برادەرترین برا و برادەرم، سەروەر!

من لەگەڵ تۆ
لە ئاستانە و دوڕیانەکاندا، لە چایخانەکاندا گەلێک ئەشکم ڕشت؛
چاوەڕێت کردایە، داخوا
لە مانەوەی بێهوودەمانەوە
لە باوەڕی بێ بەڵگەمانەوە- بە ژیان، بە خۆشبەختیی موستەحیل
چی سەوز دەبوو؟!

---

*سەروەر ئەحمەد: برادەرترین و براترین برا و برادەرم بوو، چیرۆکنووسێکی هونەرمەند؛ لە
مانگی دیسەمبەری ١٩٨٥، خۆی و دەزگیرانەکەی بەیان، پێکرا، خۆیان فڕێ دایە ڕووباری
دیجلەوە.
سەروەر تەنیا یەک کۆمەڵە چیرۆکی لەدووای خۆی جێهێشت: دخان الغرفه.

44

You Should Have Waited, Sarwar!

You should have waited, Sarwar!
You should have waited,
I wonder what might have sprouted between your dewy lips and the
    morning's!

You should have waited: I wonder, what might have sprouted
where we buried the rotted bodies of our wounds on those rusted evenings
in place of those ruins?

You should have waited:
I wonder, what might have sprouted
on the lichened stones where we laid our weary heads
during the night watch?

You should have waited
You, my brotherliest brother, my friendliest brother, and my friend, Sarwar!

You and I
at the thresholds and crossroads, in the chaixanas, I wept so much.
You should have waited, to find out
what might have sprouted
from our futile existence,
from our groundless beliefs—in life, in some impossible happiness?!

بێ هیواکان

ئێوارەیه، له شەقامەکاندا، دەستیان لەناو گیرفانی پاڵتۆ
دەگەڕێنەوه: بێ هیواکان.

ئێوارەیه، له شەقامەکاندا، قورسایی خەفەت شانی داگرتوون
بەدەم خەیاڵ و بیرکردنەوه، به خۆیان دەڵێن: ژیان چییه، بۆ چی دەژیین؟!
دەگەڕێنەوه: بێ هیواکان.

ئێوارەیه، له شەقامەکاندا، ڕۆحیان لەناو عەرەبانەی منداڵێکدا
چاویان له ئاسۆ دوورەدەسته ئاوابووەکاندا
دڵیشیان له شاری جوانییەکاندا لێ بەجێما
دەگەڕێنەوه: بێ هیواکان.

ئێوارەیه، له شەقامەکاندا
عیشقی پاکیان چەند تنۆکی سپیاتیی لینج بوو
له پاڵ وەهمێکی ڕاکشاوی ڕووباریندا هەڵوەری، تکا.

دەستیان لەناو گیرفانی پاڵتۆ، دەگەڕێنەوه بێ هیواکان.

The Hopeless

It's evening, in the streets, their hands in their coat pockets,
they return: the hopeless.

It's evening, in the streets, sadness weighs on their shoulders.
While thinking and daydreaming, they ask themselves: what is life, what are
    we living for?!
They return: the hopeless.

It's evening, in the streets, their souls on a cart pushed by a child,
their eyes on the distant horizon,
and their hearts left behind in the city of beauty.
They return: the hopeless.

It's evening, in the streets,
their pure love was a few drops of sticky whiteness
that withered, dripping beside a reclining, riverlike illusion.

Their hands in their coat pockets, the hopeless return.

گورگی پاریس

پێم دەڵێن گورگی پاریس، کەچی
من تەنیا منداڵێک بووم زوو لە دایکم جیابوومەوە.

بەیانی، نیوەڕۆ، ئێوارەکان لەسەر شانم
سەر ئاسمان نەما، ژێر زەمین نەما
جادە و کۆڵان و ژێر پەیکەرە بەرزەکان، قاوەخانە، باڕ، ژوورە پیسەکان،
سەندەویچخانە گەرەلاوژێکان، فارگۆنە تاریک و درێژەکانی ناو
شەمەندەفەرە ڕاکردووەکان..
هیچ شوێنێ نەما تێیدا نەڕەتێم؛ نەگرییم.

ئەمشەویش دیسان جێگام نییە تێیدا بخەوم
دەچم لە باری ئیسپانییەکان تا بێداربوونەوەی بەندەر و پارە و پاپۆڕەکان
دادەنیشم:
ئاه لەو چاوە شەرابییە پڕ هەوەسانە! ئاه لەو باڵا سەما سەرمەستەی
ئەو گۆرانییە شەهوەتاوییەی ئەو ژێر زەمینە دووکەڵاوییە زندانکراوە!

حەز و هەوەس و خۆشەویستی
شەو و ڕۆژ بێدار
                              ر
                          وو
                      ب
                  ا
              ر
          ى
      س
  ێ
ن
ه
وەک پێلی هەوەس بەناو پاریس دا شەپۆل دەدا..

The Wolf of Paris

They call me The Wolf of Paris, but
I was just a child separated too soon from my mother.

Morning, noon, and evenings on my shoulders,
there is no sky left, no place underground,
streets, alleys and beneath tall statues, cafes, bars, dirty rooms,
bustling sandwich shops, the long dark cars of fleeing trains.
There is no place left where I have not been exhausted, where I have not cried.

Tonight, once more, I have no place to sleep.
I go and sit at Spanish bars until the the port, with its money and ships,
    wakes up:
oh, those lustful wine-colored eyes! Oh, that drunken dancing wisp,
that lustful song from the smoke imprisoned underground!

Desire and lust and love,
awake day and night,
the
        S
           E
              I
                  N
                      E
                          R
                              I
                                  V
                                      E
                                            R
              like waves of lust, it lurches through Paris . . .

کەچی پێم دەڵێن گورگی پاریس
منیش تەنیا، مندالێک بووم زوو لە دایکم جیا بوومەوە.

لە باغی لووگزەمبوورگ دەمەوئێواران هەست بە تەنیاییەکی کوشنده دەکەم
نیوەشەوانیش، باڕ و باخچه و شەقامەکان
لێم دەبنه پۆلی گۆرانی و بەسەر کەپۆلی تەنیاییمەوە هەڵدەنیشن
دەنووک لە برینی هەستی بۆگەنبووی ئاوارەیی و بێکەسیم دەدەن.

شەوان و شەقام، شەوان و جگەره، شەوان و عارەق، شەوان و بەرمیله پڕ
لە زبڵ، دەرپێ، بووکه شووشەی شکاو، شەوان و ماست، میوه ڕزیوه
سەرخۆشەکان، شەوان و گۆرانی، شەوان و گازینۆی شەوانی هەولێر،
شەوان و پیربالْ، شەوان و مێۆژ، شەوان و چیرۆکه دریژەکانی میمکه
زلێخا، شەوان و شار، شەقامه بەهەشتییه هێمنەکانی، ڕیشۆلەکانی،
چیا، قاسپەی کەو، بەسەر کۆتی بەناو دەشتی دەنووک زەردا ڕۆیشتن،
سەیرکردنه زەرگ لە خۆدانی دەرویشە قژ دریژەکانی بەر تەکیەکان،
گەمه و گۆلمەز و هەڵبەزینەوەی دلْخۆشی سەر گرد و تەپۆلکه
رەنگینەکان، پرتەقال دزینی گەڕەکی ناوقەسران، بێچووه کەرویشک،
کورتەک و شەروالی تازەی سپێدانی جەژن، چوکلێت، قشپۆخی، فلیمی
کارتۆن، بن لەیلووگەکان، پاسکیل، پیاسه، ئاو...
من هیچم نەدیت. هیچم نەدیت. هیچم نەدیت.
گەنجیتیشم، حەیف، ئەوەتا: سالْانی سەفەر
سالْانی هەمیشه مالْ گوێزانەوە
سالْانی کتێبخانه و متبەق بە کۆلی
سالْانی کورت: تەنیا سێ ڕۆژ، یان شەوێک و بەس.
سالْانی ئۆتۆستۆپ
سالْانی ماندوو
سالْانی فینگەر چیپس.

پێم دەڵێن گورگی پاریس، کەچی
من تەنیا مندالێک بووم زوو لە دایکم جیابوومەوە.

So they call me the Wolf of Paris.
I was just a child separated too soon from my mother.

Near evening, I feel a deadly loneliness in the Jardin du Luxembourg.
At midnight, the bars, parks and streets—
they become a flock of songs and perch on the shoulderblades of my
    loneliness.
They peck the wound of my putrid feelings of displacement and loneliness.

Nights and streets, nights and cigarettes, nights and arak, nights and barrels
    full of garbage, panties, broken dolls, nights and yogurt, drunken rotten
    fruit, nights and songs,
nights and nighttime casinos of Hewlêr, nights and Pirbal, nights and raisins,
    nights and Aunt Zulaikha's long stories, nights and the city, its quiet
    heavenly streets, its starlings, mountains, the coo of a partridge, walking
    on the dirt, across the withered grass of the yellow-beaked plains,
    watching the long-haired dervishes in front of the tekyes skewering
    themselves, playing and climbing and happy jumps on the colorful hills,
    stealing oranges in Naw Qesran, leverets, the new kurtas and shalwars
    of Eid mornings, chocolate, candies, cartoons, beneath the swings, a
    bicycle, walking, water . . .
I didn't see anything. I didn't see anything. I didn't see anything.
My youth, alas, here: years of travel
years of constant moving
years of my library and kitchen on my shoulders
short years: Just three days, or one night and that's all.
The hitchhiking years
the weary years
the years of French fries.

They call me The Wolf of Paris, but
I was only a child separated too soon from my mother.

لە بەندەرە مەمک پەمبە ساردەکانی ئەستمبۆڵەوە
تا بەر حەوشەی کاتێدراڵە پیرۆزەکەی سانتیاگۆ
بستی زەویی میهرەبانم نەدۆزییەوە کە خەونەکانمی تیا بڕوێنم؛
لەسەر شۆستە زێڕەوشانەکانی دیمەشقەوە
تا چیمەن و قەراغ ڕووبارە ڕەنگینەکانی سنێگەستین هیچ باوەشێکم
نەدۆزییەوە
کە داڵدەی تەنیایی و بێکەسیم بدا.

لەندەن		ستۆکهۆڵم		وارشۆ		کۆپنهاگن
		توولۆوز		مۆناکۆ		بەرشەلۆنە

کەچی هەمیشە تەنیا
چەند شەقامێک، چەند باخچەیەک و قاوەخانەیەک
یا ناونوێنێکی نامۆی ساردی شەوێک و... بەس!

ئاخ، لە چ سەرزەمینێکی ئەفسانەییدا مندالّیی خۆم بدۆزمەوە!
لە چ خەونێکی ئەفیوونیدا نیشتیمانێکی دیکە بنیات بنێم
با بە ئەندازەی تەنیا حەوشەکەمان بێ
با بە ئەندازەی تەنیا ژێر درەختێکی باخچەکەشمان بێ؛
یان بە ئەندازەی تەنیا کورسیەک
لە چایخانەیەکی دووکەلّاویی کەرە گوندێکی شارەزوور دا!!

لێرە:
شەوەکان، ڕۆژەکان، سالّەکان... بەسەردەچن؛
کەچی ژیان، هەمیشە تەنیا
لە دەرگادانی دەمەوئێوارەیەکی ڕاکشاوی زەردی یەکشەمووانە:
کاتێ دوو ڕووخسار، دوو ڕووخساری تا بلّێی تینوو، تا بلّێی ماندوو،
بە زەردەخەنەیەکی کەیفخۆشەوە بە یەکتر دەلّێن: "ئێوارە باش."
زرن   زرن   زرن   زرنگانەوەی   زەنگی
سەعاتی زیوینی دلّبلّندی سەر دیواری کلّێساکان
بەو دەنگە پیرە جارسکەرەی خۆیانەوە، گشت ئێوارەیەک
تالّێکی دیکە لە قژی سەرم سپی دەکەن.

52

From the cold pink breasts of Istanbul's ports
to the plaza of the Holy Cathedral of Santiago
I found no kind handful of land where I could plant my dreams;
from the golden sidewalks of Damascus
to the grassy shores of beautiful Snekkersten I found no embrace
to shelter my loneliness and abandonment.
Copenhagen   Warsaw   Stockholm   London
Barcelona   Monaco   Toulouse
but always lonely
a few streets, a few parks and a coffee shop
or a strange cold bed for one night and . . . that's all!

Oh, in what mythical land may I find my childhood!
In what opium dream may I build another homeland
let it only be the size of our yard
let it even be just the measure of the shade our tree casts in the garden;
or just the size of a chair
in the smoky tea shop of a deaf village in Sharazur!

Here:
nights, days, years . . . pass by;
but life is always just
the knocking on a door on a reclined yellow Sunday evening:
when two faces, two faces with such thirst, such exhaustion,
say to each other with a cheerful smile: "Good evening."
Ding   ding   ding   the ringing of the
lofty silver clocks on the churches' faces
with their old jarring voices, every evening
they whiten another strand of my hair.

هەرچی چاویکی میهرەبان و جوان ببینم پێی دەڵێم ئاه دایکی شیرینم
هەرچی وەهمێکی ناوقەدباریک و کوک ببینم پێی دەڵێم ئاه، دەزگیرانەکەم!

من بە بارتەقای هەموو گەردوون برسیم
من بە بارتەقای هەموو گەردوون غەریبیی مندالّی و
گەرەکە دووره بەهەشتییه ویّرانکراوەی خۆمان دەکەم
بەلّام حەیفێک و سیّ سەد مخابن: من واوەیلا و نالّه و خوێنم وەبیردێتەوه
وەی سالّی سەربرانان
بۆمباران و گوللەپرژانی ناو حەوشەکەمان
ئێواره بوو
من و دایکم، له گەراجێکی شلّەژاودا ڕاوەستابووین
دایکم هۆن — هۆن ورده فرمێسکی دادەباراند؛
دوواین ئاوازی غەمگینی لێوی بەخشییه زەردیی ڕوومەتەکانم گوتی:
"کوڕم ناتبینمەوه. خوا ئاگادارت بیّ!"
ئەوسات تەمەنم تەنیا چوار-پێنج خەم و خەفەت بوو.
من زوو له دایکم جیابوومەوه.

Every kind and beautiful pair of eyes I see, I say to them, "Oh, my sweet
    mother"
whenever I see a narrow-waisted and deserving illusion, I say to them, "Oh,
    my fiancée!"

I am as hungry as the entire universe
I miss my childhood and our faraway destroyed heavenly neighborhood
as much as the entire universe
but a pity and three hundred misfortunes: I remember the woe and the cry
    and the blood
oh year of slaughter
it was raining bombs and bullets in our yard
it was evening
my mother and I were standing in a confused garage
my mother shed one tear after another;
she gave the last sad melody of her lips to the yellowness of my cheeks and
    said:
"I won't see you again, son. May God keep you!"
At the time, I was only four or five grief-years old.
I separated from my mother too soon.

خلوود

خلوود خلوود خلوود "خلوود" خلوود خلوود خلوود خلوود خلوود "خلوود" و خلوود خلوود خلوود خلوود خلوود؟ خلوود خلوود خلوود خلوود خلوود خلوود! خلوود خلوود خلوود، خلوود، خلوود خلوود خلوود، خلوود: خلوود خلوود خلوود خلوود (خلوود) خلوود وهل ل، خلوود؟ خلوود؟

خلــوود

خلــوود

خلــوود

خلــوود

خلــوود

خلــوود

خلــوود

خلــوود

خلــوود

خلــوود

.. خ ل وخلــوود، و د ...

Immortality

Key:

خلود (*khulud*) means "immortality" or "perpetuity" in Arabic, and is used as a female given name.

بیۆگرافی

دایکم مرد و بەیەكجاری بەجێی هێشتم
دەزگیرانم ‑دوای سەفەری لەناكاوم‑
گری بەردا گیانی خۆی و بووه زووخاڵ
خوشك و برا و هاوڕێكانیشم
یا ئاگری جەنگ و بۆمبا بارانەكان هەڵی لووشین
یا هەر یەكە و پەرتەوازەی وڵاتێك بوون و ئێستا ناونیشانی هیچیان نازانم.

لە خۆم غەریبێ، لە خۆم بێكەسێ
خاتوو زولەیخا تەنیا زستانێك لە ماڵی خۆی حەواندومیەوه
میرسلۆڤیا تەنیا بەهارێك بووه لانه و نیشتمانم
ئیسپیغانسا تەنیا مانگێك بووه یار و دەزگیرانم
سیمۆنا: چەند هەفتەیەك
ئەنژلیك: سێ‑چوار شەوی سپی
غووزین: شەوێك
ئانكا: شەوێك
بەیاتریس، بەیاتریسی میهرەبانیش:
تەنیا سەعاتێك
سەعاتێك و... بەس.

من دەزانم: سەرزەمینی جاویدانی
سەرزەمینی هەمیشه جوان و میهرەبانی
لەودیو سنووری ماچ و باوەش و ژووانەكانه
لەودیو سنووری ڕۆژگارەكانه.

ئاه ئەی یار
وەره، ژووانێكم لەودیو سنووری ڕۆژگارەكان بدەرێ!

Biography

My mother died and left me forever
my fiancée—after my sudden journey—
set fire to her own body and turned into coal
my sisters, brothers, and friends
were either devoured by the fire of war and rain of bombs
or dispersed to different countries and now I don't know any of their
    addresses.

A stranger to myself, a lonely man am I
Miss Zulaikha comforted me for just one winter in her house
Miroslavia became my den and homeland for just one spring
Esperanza became my lover and fiancée for just one month
Simona: several weeks
Angelique: three or four white nights
Ghusin: one night
Anka: one night
Beatrice, kind Beatrice:
just one hour
only . . . an hour.

I know: the immortal land
the land of infinite beauty and kindness is
beyond the border of kisses and embraces and trysts
beyond the borders of a day.

Ah, my love,
come, let's go on a date beyond the borders of a day!

١٩٩١-١٩٧٤

من
هەرچی شار و
گوند و
هەرچی باخچه و گەڕەک و
ڕەز و کۆڵان و
هەرچی مندالْ و ڕووبار و شەقام و
مێردمندالْ و ئەستێرەیەکی پەنجەرەیەکی
کوڕ و کچ و قەیرەکچ و ژنێکی شۆخی... خۆشم ویستن:
ئاخ!
گەردەلوولێکی
ئەرژەنگی خوێنین
هەلْی لووشین.

1974–1991

each city and

        town and

each garden and   neighborhood and

     vineyard and   subdivision and

each child and   river and   street and

     teenager and   star and   window

boy and   girl and   spinster and   pretty woman . . .   that I loved:

agh!

a hurricane

bestial and bloody

devoured them.

EXIL

لەو ئاسمانە میهرەبانەدا

نیشتیمانێکی هەمیشەیی ئاسوودەم هەیە،

لە شەقامە ئاوارەکانیشدا

مشتێ ئاواز و بۆن و لەززەت.

لە نێوان ئاسمان و شەقامەکاندا، ڕۆژگارەکانم

بێهوودانە

بەسەر دەچن...

EXIL

Up in that kind sky

I have a permanent, comfortable homeland,

and down on the exiled streets

a handful of melody, scent, and taste.

Between the sky and the streets, my days

pass

vainly by . . .

خانوو به کۆڵ

ڕێگاکان
ڕێگاکان
ڕێگاکان
هیچیان نەماون پێیاندا نەڕۆم.

مالّەکان
مالّەکان
مالّەکان
هیچیان نەماون تێیاندا نەمرم.

تۆ، ئەی ئەوەی کە پەنجەکانت ڕێ پیشاندەری تیشکی خۆر و ڕێی دەریایە!
من لە هەر چی ڕێیەک هەیە زۆر بێزارم
من لە هەر چی مالّێک هەیە زۆر بێزارم؛
تۆ –
تۆ ڕێگایەک
بە منی تەڕوەنە پیشان بدە
تۆ خانوویەک بە منی بێ مالّ پیشان بدە؛
تۆ، ئەی ئەوەی کە پەنجەکانت ڕێ پیشاندەری تیشکی خۆر و ڕێی دەریایە!

ئۆسپانهۆف: ١٩٨٥

My Home on My Shoulders

paths
paths
paths
there's no path I haven't crossed.

homes
homes
homes
there's no home I haven't died in.

you, the one whose fingers point to the sun's rays and the sea's path!
I am fed up with every path
I am fed up with every home;
you—
you show a path
to me, the shrub that blocks it
you show a house to a homeless man;
you, the one whose fingers point to the sun's rays and the sea's path!

Ospanov: 1985

ژ

بیری

قاڵدرمەی

ناو حەوشەکەمان

دەکەم

کە دەیگەیاندمەوە

ژووره

بەرزەکەم

...

J

i

   miss

      the stairs

         in our courtyard

            that took me to

               my room

                  up there

                     ...

سپیاتییەکانی ناو رەش

رەشاییەکانی ناو سپی

١٩٩٩

The Whiteness in the Blackness
The Blackness in the Whiteness
1999

بیرەوەرییەکانی دوورەوڵاتیم

١٩٨٤: کاتێ ئازاری شکۆمەندم، دەمەوعەسران، لە شەقامەکانی تاران پیاسەی دەکرد، چلّکی سەدەکانی ناوەڕاستی لەسەر دەنیشت، ئێوارانیش: ماندوو، بە بەردەم "میدان ذوب آهن" بەرەو ئۆردووگای "بیست و پێنج هەزار مەیتە ئاسوودەکە" لە کەرەج دەگەڕایەوە.

١٩٨٥: قاچی ڕاستم لە دیمەشق برسێتی دەیخوارد، قاچی چەپیشم لە بەرلینی ڕۆژهەڵات: سەگی پۆلیسی.

١٩٨٦: "پەنیرێکی بۆگەنی سارد" خەریک بوو سەرتاپای ڕۆحم ژەهراوی بکات. کیەرکۆگارد ڕزگاری کردم.

١٩٨٧: سەرپشتی کەشتییەکەی ڕێگای ستۆکهۆڵم-کڕاکۆڤ تاقە حەشارگەیەکی ژیان بوو.

١٩٨٨: هەموو ئێوارەیەک لە قاوەخانەکانی ڤیشی و بیزەنسۆن و گرۆنۆبڵ و مۆنتی کارلۆ، شەراب یان قاوەم لەگەڵ پۆل ئێلوار و ژاک بغیل و ئاراگۆن و بلیز ساندرا دەخواردەوە.

١٩٨٩: جگەرگۆشەکانم: کاکۆڵ زێڕین، فەردەپەتاتەی ژەهراوییان بەسەردا دەکەوت و کەڵەواژ دەبوونەوە. لەسەر سنووری بەهەشت-دۆزەخدا نۆ هەزار و نۆسەدونۆ گۆڕی بچکۆلەم بۆ کۆرپەکانی خۆم هەڵکەند؛ ئێستا لەسەر گۆڕی هەر یەکێکیان حاجی لەقلەقێک سەوز بووە.

١٩٩٠: لەگەڵ سەرۆکی دەوڵەتی فەرەنسا، فرانسوا میتران، بە شەڕ هاتم و مالّی UNم بەردباران کرد.

١٩٩١: قەڵەمەکەم لە ئەرشیفخانەی SOAS، جەنتاکەم لە مالّی مارگرێت دووراس، قاچم لە باخچەکانی مالّی ژان ژاک ڕۆسۆ، چاویشم لە گەڵەرییەکانی شەقامی سێن کەوتبوون.

١٩٩٢: عبدالقادر الجنانی بە ئەندرێ بڕۆتۆن و فیلیپ سووپۆی ناساندم، وتی: "ئێوە پێویستە ببنە برادەر."

My Memories of Exile

1984: When my noble pain strolled the streets of Tehran in the afternoon, the grimy sediment of the Middle Ages fell over it. And at dusk, exhausted, I passed the "Twenty Thousand Happy Corpses" Camp in Karaj.

1985: In Damascus, hunger ate my right foot, and in East Berlin the police dogs ate my left.

1986: "A rank cold cheese" almost poisoned my entire soul. Kierkegaard saved me.

1987: The Stockholm-Kraków ferry was my only refuge in life.

1988: Every afternoon in the cafes of Vichy and Besançon and Grenoble and Monte Carlo I drank wine or coffee with Éluard and Brel and Aragon and Cendrars.

1989: My babies: their golden hair, the sacks of poisonous potatoes crushed them and they died. At the Paradise-Hell border I dug nine thousand nine hundred and ninety-nine tiny graves for my babies; now, atop every one of their tombs, a stork has sprouted.

1990: I fought with the President of France, François Mitterrand, and I threw stones at the UN headquarters.

1991: My pen in the archives at SOAS, my briefcase at Marguerite Duras' house, my feet in Jean-Jacques Rousseau's gardens, and my eyes in the galleries on Rue de Seine.

1992: Abdel Kader El-Janabi introduced me to André Breton and Philippe Soupault, and said: "You should be friends."

۱۹۹۳: دەستی چەپم فرۆشت، بۆ ئەوەی بتوانم چاوێکی ئیتالی بکرم، قاچی راستم فرۆشت، بۆ ئەوەی بتوانم گوێچکەیەکی ئینگلیزی بکرم، رەشاییەکانی پرچی خۆم فرۆشت، بۆ ئەوەی بتوانم کتێبێکی فەرەنسی بکرم.

۱۹۹٤: هەموو عارەقەی گیانی خۆم فرۆشت، بۆ ئەوەی بتوانم بلیتێکی گەڕانەوە بۆ هەولێر بکرم.

1993: I sold my left hand to buy an Italian eye. I sold my right foot to buy an English ear. I sold the black hairs on my head to buy a French book.

1994: I sold all the sweat in my body to buy a return ticket to Hewlêr.

٤٤ پێناسه بۆ دوورەوڵاتی

١. گەردەلوولێک بتبا.

٢. گاستینێکی قەرەباڵغ، مندالێکی نۆ ساڵانەی لێ بێتە ژوورێ که له زمانی هیچ کەسێک و هیچ شتێکی ئەوێ تێنەگات.

٣. دۆزەخ.

٤. Metamorphose

٥. خۆڵه خۆ گۆڕان، خۆ لێ گۆڕان.

٦. دڵی له جمان نەکەوتووی داهێنان.

٧. زەبوونی و چاوشۆڕی و هەست به کەمی کردن.

٨. زەبوونییەکی زەبوون، چاوشۆڕییەکی چاوشۆڕ، هەست به کەمی کردنێکی کەم.

٩. غەریبیکردنی دراوسێکەتان.

١٠. به تاقی تەنیا، به دڵێکی پڕ له هەستی غەریبی و تەنیاییەوە، بێ پارە و پووڵ، له کامپۆ سانتا مارگریتا حەز بکەی بگریی.

١١. حەز بکەی سەرتاپای خزم و کەسوکاری کوردستانت بۆ بگوازنەوە بۆ نزیک ماڵەکەت له گەڕەکی ئۆکسفۆرد، له لەندەن.

١٢. له ئێرانەوە، هەر به پێ، ڕابکەیت، تا دەگەیتە چین.

١٣. سێزده چەقۆ له ژنێکی دانیمارکی بدەیت: لەبەر ئەوەی لێت جودا دەبێتەوە و پشت له گرێ چینییەکەت دەکات.

١٤. تەنیایی، تەنیایی، تەنیایی...

١٥. نیوەشەوێک، باوەشکردن به درەختێکی تەنیای سەرشەقامێک.

١٦. پیری.

١٧. جورئەتی ئەوەت نەبێ تەماشای ناوچاوی هەرزەکارێکی تورەهاتی ئەڵمانی بکەیت!

١٨. قەمسەڵەی دەستی دووەمی دزراوی دەست پەناهەندە لوبنانییەکان، به نرخێکی نیوەقیمەت بکڕیتەوە.

١٩. له کۆپنهاگن، به کەترە ژنێکی پیری ناشرینی له مێرد دابڕاوی پۆڵەندی بڵێی: "پێخۆشحاڵم به ناسینت!"

٢٠. له ستۆکهۆڵم سواری شەمەندەفەر بیت، به دوای کچەقەرەجێکی سەماکەری سێرک بچیته هەنگاریا، گەڵەسیۆز، لەوێ ناونیشانەکەی نەدۆزیتەوە و بگریت.

٢١. نیوەشەوان، له گەرمەی خەو ڕابچلەکیت و بۆ دایکت بگریت.

44 Definitions of Exile

1. A hurricane carrying you away.
2. A crowded square, a nine-year-old arriving, not understanding anyone's language or anything else there.
3. Hell.
4. *Metamorphose.*
5. Transforming, changing completely.
6. The heart beating without pausing for imagination.
7. Misery, shame, insecurity.
8. Such miserable misery, such shameful shame, such insecure insecurity.
9. Missing your neighbor.
10. So alone, heart brimming with loneliness and the sense of being strange, without a single real, on the verge of tears in Campo Santa Margherita.
11. Wishing for all your family and relatives from Kurdistan to move nearby your house in Oxford Circus, in London.
12. From Iran, by foot, running till you reach China.
13. Stabbing a Danish woman thirteen times because she leaves you, turning her back on your Chinese complex.
14. Loneliness, loneliness, loneliness . . .
15. One midnight, embracing a tree alone on the street.
16. Old age.
17. Not daring link eyes with a useless German teenager!
18. Buying a secondhand coat stolen by Lebanese refugees for half price.
19. Telling a decayed, ugly, divorced old Polish woman in Copenhagen, "How nice to meet you!"
20. Boarding a train in Stockholm, going to Gelasias, Hungary, to find a Romani ballerina in the circus, but not finding her address and crying.
21. In the middle of the night, startling awake from the depths of dreaming and crying for your mother.

٢٢. نەخۆشیی بەردەوام بەردەوام بەردەوامی   چاوەڕێکردنی نامە.

٢٢. حەزکردنی بەردەوام بەردەوام بەردەوامی   نووسینی نامە.

٢٣. سنووری ئەڵمانیا بەرەو هۆڵەندا، یان هیی پۆڵۆنیا بەرەو سوێد، بە پێی ببڕیت و وا بزانی کە ئیتر سەقام دەگریت و ئاسوودەیی ڕووت تێ دەکا

٢٤. دڵ لە دڵ دانی ئێوارانی یەکشەمووان، ئایا بچی بە تەنیا لە باڕیک دابنیشیت، یان نا؟

٢٥. ئیرەیی ببەی بە سەگێکی نەرویجی.

٢٦. خۆت فڕێ بدەیتە ژێر شەمەندەفەرێکی ناو توولەبانەی ستۆکهۆڵم و هیچیشت لێ نەیەت.

٢٧. بەڕازی ڕەش.

٢٨. لە ناوەڕاستی مەیدانی ڤیستەپۆڕت، لە کۆپنهاگن، سەعات دووانزە و نیوی شەو بە سەرخۆشی، بە کوردی هاوار بکەیت: "ئای چەندم خۆش دەوێ."

٢٩. حەز بکەی تەنانەت باوەش بە ئایدز بیشدا بکەیت: تەنیا بۆ ئەوەی هەست بە سۆزێک بکەیت و تەنیاییت بڕەوێتەوە.

٣٠. خۆزگەی ئەوەت بێ نەورۆز زوو دابێت، بۆ ئەوەی لەگەڵ کوردەکان کۆ ببیتەوە.

٣١. چاوەڕێکردنی بەردەوامی بەردەوامی ئێوارانی یەکشەمووان.

٣٢. "لە ئەستەمبۆڵ، بە روتبە و نیشانە و ئەعزایەتیی مەجلیسی عالییەوە لە 'ئوططە' کە مەڵبەندی پرەنسەکانی کۆنی ڕۆم بوو، لە قەسرێکی مومتازدا دائەنیشتم، کە شەو ئەنوستم، لە خەوما: لە گورگەدەر، لە باخەکەی شێخ ئەحمەدی زلێخا هەنارم ئەدزی."

پیرەمێرد: **ژین**، ژ ٨٩٤، ت ٢/١٩٤٧

٣٣. ئایرش بار، لە ستۆکهۆڵم، لە بەرلین، لە کۆپنهاگن، لە لەندەن.

٣٤. مندالێک بیت و هەست بکەی لەناو حەشاماتێکی گەورەدا لە دایکت دابڕاویت.

٣٥. پیرەژنێکی بە ڕەسەن جوولەکەی پورتوگالی، لە پاریس، بەزەیی بە حاڵتدا بێتەوە و پێت بڵی: "تۆ بۆچی ناگەڕێیتەوە وڵاتی خۆت؟"

٣٦. سیزدە ساڵان مەنفا و دەربەدەرییەکەی عەرەبی شەمۆ لە سیبیریا.

٣٧. لە فڕۆکەخانەی دیمەشق بتەوێ تەیارەیەک بتەقێنیتەوە.

٣٨. هەژدە مانگ بە کوردی قسە نەکەیت و لە داخی دەردی بێوڵاتی لە ئەوروووپا. وەک شەریف پاشا، داخی دڵی خۆت بە کچ و ژنە ئەورووپییەکان هەڵبڕێژیت.

22. The sickness of waiting always, always, always   for a letter.

22. Wanting always, always, always   to write letters.

23. Walking across the border between Germany and Holland, or between Poland and Switzerland, and thinking you will settle there and your happiness will return to you.

24. The doubts of every Sunday afternoon: whether to sit alone at a bar or not?

25. Envying a Norwegian dog.

26. Throwing yourself beneath a train in a Stockholm tunnel but nothing happening to you.

27. *Black pig.*

28. In the middle of Vesterbros Torv, in Copenhagen, at twelve-thirty at night, drunk, belting out in Kurdish: "Oh how I love her."

29. Wishing even to embrace AIDS: just to experience some passion and lose your sense of loneliness.

30. Wishing that Nawroz would come early, so you could meet up with other Kurds.

31. Waiting always, always, always on Sunday afternoons.

32. "In Istanbul, with rank and insignia and being a member of the high tribunal, in Otta which was the territory of the princesses of old Turkey, I lived in a luxurious palace. At night when I slept, in my dreams, in the village of Gurgadar, in the garden of Sheikh Ahmad Zileha, I stole pomegranates."

—Piramerd, *Zheen*, No. 894, 2/1947

33. Irish Bar in Stockholm, in Berlin, in Copenhagen, in London.

34. A child who feels lost in a crowd, separated from his mother.

35. A Portuguese Jewish old lady in Paris pitying your state: "Why don't you return to your country?"

36. Arab Shamo's thirteen years of exile and displacement in Siberia.

37. In the Damascus airport, wanting to blow up a plane.

38. Not speaking Kurdish for eighteen months and with the shame of being stateless, in Europe, like Sharif Pasha, unloading your pain on the European girls and women.

۳۹. له لەندەن، له قاتی یازدەهەمی ئاپارتمانێکەوه خۆت توور هەڵبدەیته خوارەوە.

٤٠. غەریبیکردنی عەفیفه ئەسکەندەر و ڕەسووڵ گەردی و جاربەجاریش حمدیه سالح و بناتها.

٤١. وا بزانیت مەنفا و غەریبییەکەی حاجی قادری کۆیی له چاو ئەوەی تۆ گەمەی مندالان بووه.

٤٢. باوەش به دارێکدا بکەیت: وا بزانیت دەزگیرانته.

٤٣. حەشیشەکێشان و خۆتەسلیمکردنه تەنوویمی و موگناتیسی: بەس بۆ ئەوەی تەنیا جارێک "ژوورەکەی خۆت" ببینیتەوە.

٤٤. دوای حەشیشەکێشان ومەستبوونێکی بەنگ، سوێند به چل و چوار پێغەمبەران بخۆیت که به ڕاستی، بوویتەته پێغەمبەر!

39. In London, throwing yourself onto the street from an apartment's eleventh floor.

40. Missing Afifa Iskander and Rasul Gardi and sometimes Hamdiya Salih and *her girls*.

41. Thinking that the exile and displacement of Haji Qadir Koyi was child's play compared to yours.

42. Hugging a tree and thinking it's your fiancée.

43. Smoking hashish and giving in to hypnosis: only so you can see "your own room again."

44. After smoking hashish and intoxicating yourself with bhang, swearing by the forty-four prophets that you truly have become one of them!

پەمبەترین
ئامۆژگارییەکان
لەبارەی
مۆر

لە ژنێڤ، بەرێککەوت، ژان ژاک رۆسۆم بینی؛ وتی:
"هانێ دان پیانانەکانم، ببیە؛
لای خۆتان بیکە بە باخچە."

لە پاریس، بەرێککەوت، ڤۆڵتێرم بینی؛ وتی:
"هانێ ئەوەتا ورێنەکانم، بیانبە؛
لای خۆتان بیانکە بە قانوون."

لە ستۆکهۆڵم، بەرێککەوت، ستریندبێرگم بینی؛ وتی:
"هانێ ئەوەتا رقبوونەوەم لە ژن، ببیە؛
لای خۆتان بیکە بە مۆنالیزا."

لە رۆکێن، بەرێککەوت، نیتشەم بینی، وتی:
"هانێ ئەوەتا شێتیم، ببیە؛
لای خۆتان بیکە بە سەوزەگیا."

لە قورتوبە، بەرێککەوت، هەمەنگوام بینی؛ وتی:
"هانێ ئەوەتا خۆکوشتنم، ببیە؛
لای خۆتان بیکە بە ژیان."

The Pinkest
Advice
about
Purple

In Geneva, I bumped into Jean-Jacques Rousseau; he said,
"Here are my *Confessions*, take them—
back in your homeland, turn them into a garden."

In Paris, I bumped into Voltaire; he said,
"Here are my blabberings, take them—
back in your homeland, turn them into law."

In Stockholm, I bumped into Strindberg; he said,
"Here is my hatred for women, take it—
back in your homeland, turn it into the Mona Lisa.

In Röcken, I bumped into Nietzsche; he said,
"Here is my madness, take it—
back in your homeland, turn it into lush foliage."

In Córdoba, I bumped into Hemingway; he said,
"Here is my suicide, take it—
back in your homeland, turn it into a life."

سپیاتییەکانی ناو ڕەش
ڕەشاییەکانی ناو سپی

The Whiteness in the Blackness
The Blackness in the Whiteness

Key:

The underlying text is unidentified.

stone

a girl

with an orange :

the sun

melted

above your head   !

ئاسمان
...قەڵات...
..مندالیم..خانەقا..پیرباڵ..تەیراوە..گەنجیتیم..هەمین..تۆپانی..ناسک..

Hewlêr from Far Away

sky

... the castle ...

..my childhood..Khanqah..Pirbal..Tairawa..my youth..Hemin..football..Nask..

شیراتۆن لەبەر باراندا

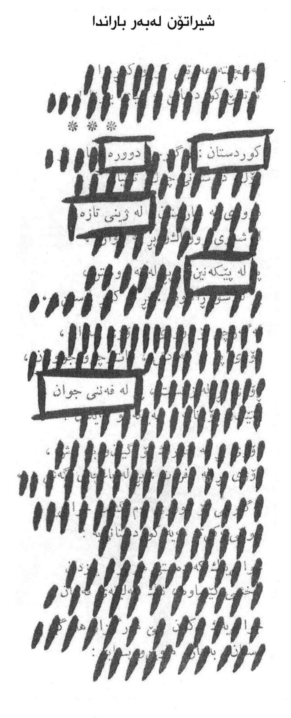

Sheraton in the Rain

Kurdistan: is far

   from new life

           from laughter

from the fine arts

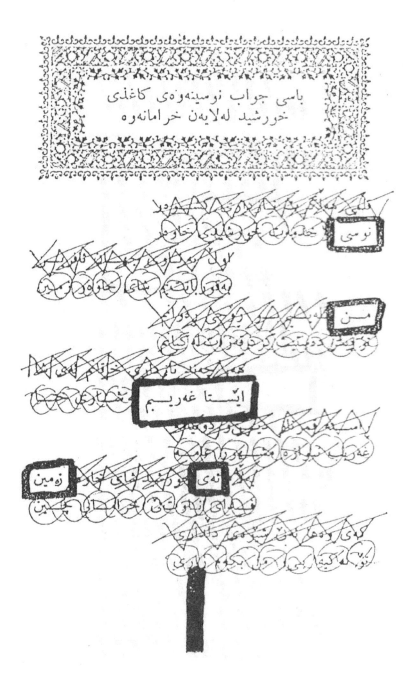

Kharaman's Discussion of Khurshid's Letter in Response

<u>Key:</u>
The title appears within the ornamental box, and the underlying text is unidentified.

she wrote

I am

now a stranger

ah   world

پەنجەرە

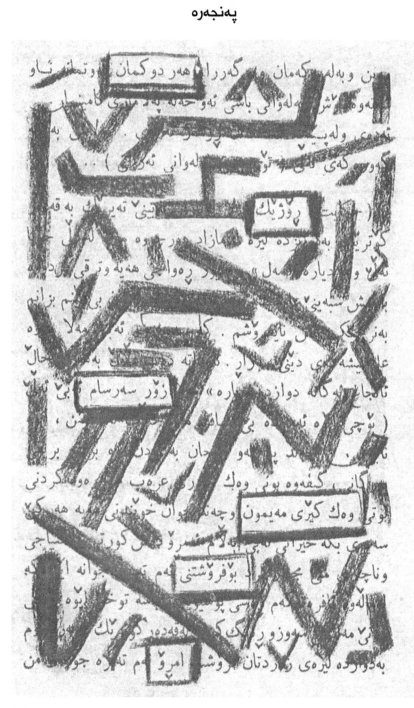

Window

both of us

one day

bewildered

like a monkey's penis

for sale

today

All of my streets
ئۆف
All of my windows
ئاخ
All of my mothers
All of my pictures
All of my chairs
All of my brothers
All of my sisters
All of my fingers

All of my birds
All of my cars
All of my goddesses
All of my lessons
All of my balls
ئازیزم
All of my papers
All of my cousins
All of my waters
All of my friends
All of my songs

ARE DEAD

English Poetry Takhmis

All of my streets
Oof
All of my windows
Agh
All of my mothers
All of my pictures
All of my chairs
All of my brothers
All of my sisters
All of my fingers

All of my birds
All of my cars
All of my goddesses
All of my lessons
All of my balls
My dear
All of my papers
All of my cousins
All of my waters
All of my friends
All of my songs

ARE DEAD

۱۹۹۳

مادام پارەی پێڵاوێک لە پاریس
۳۰ کەسی برسیی لە سیبیریا پێ تێر دەکرێ،
مادام ۳ کڕۆنی ساردی سوێدی
دەکاتە ژیانی ۳۳ ڕۆژی ۳۳ کەسی برسیی سۆماڵی،

مادام نرخی بیپسی کۆلایەک لە شیکاگۆ
دەکاتە مووچەی یەک مانگی تەواوی مووچەخۆرێکی
بێ مووچە لە هەولێر،
مادام پاوەندێک دەکاتە دوو تەنەکە بەنزین لە سارایەڤۆ،

مادام نرخی عەگالێک لە سعوودیە
دەکاتە دوو خانوو بۆ بێخانوویەکی خانەدان لە ئەرمینیا،
مادام مارکێکی ئەڵمانی دەکاتە نزیکەی قوتووە پەنیرێک و
یەک فەردە پەتاتە لە بیترسبۆرگ،

مادام نرخی دەرپێ قوتەیەک لە ژنێف
دەکاتە پازدە کورتەک و شەڵوار لە بۆمبای،

مادام دۆلارێکی حیز دەکاتە پێنج سەد دینار لە سلێمانی،
مادام تەنانەت سی پێنج سەد دیناریش ناکاتە تەنانەت
گلاسێک دۆندرمە لە ڤینیس.
دەبێ ئەم جیهانە، سەرتاسەری، وێران بکرێ!

94

1993

As long as the price of a shoe in Paris
is enough to feed 30 of the hungry in Siberia,
as long as 3 cold Swedish krona
is worth 33 days in the lives of 33 of the hungry in Somalia,

as long as the price of a Pepsi-Cola in Chicago
is worth the monthly salary of an employee
gone unpaid in Hewlêr,
as long as a pound is worth two tins of fuel in Sarajevo,

as long as the price of an agal in Saudi Arabia
is worth two houses for a homeless nobleman in Armenia,
as long as a German mark is worth almost a can of cheese
and a sack of potatoes in St. Petersburg,

as long as the price of a pair of underwear in Geneva
is worth fifteen kurta and shalwar in Bombay,

as long as the asshole dollar is worth five hundred dinars in Slemani,
as long as even thirty 500 dinars is not worth
a glass of ice cream in Venice,
this world must be destroyed—entirely!

سروودی غەریبەیەکی سەرشێنی
دەست و پێ سپی

لە تەورێز
دانەیەک گەنمم هەڵگرتەوە
گوتم: "بۆ چۆلەکەیەکی برسی دەییبەمەوە هەولێر."

لە ڕێگای نێوان یەزیلۆ و ڤینیز
دەروشانەوەی چەپکێ گڵۆپی عەلەتریکم دیت
گوتم: "دەسکەنەی دەکەم
دەییبەمەوە بۆ کۆڵانە تاریکەکانی سلێمانی.

لە شتووتگارت
جریوە جریوی ڕەنگینی پۆپەی چنارانم دیت
گوتم: "دەیانچنم
دەیانبەمەوە بۆ شەقامە غەمگینەکانی زاخۆ."

96

Song of a Blue-headed,
White-handed Stranger

In Tabriz
I collected a single grain of wheat.
I said to myself: "I will take it back to a hungry sparrow in Hewlêr."

On the road between Yazello and Venice
I saw the gleam of a bouquet of electric lights.
I said to myself: "I will pick them by hand
and take them back to Slemani's dark alleys."

In Stuttgart
I saw the colorful crowns of the willows chirping.
I said to myself: "I will collect them
and take them back to Zakho's blue streets."

Apprivoise-moi

ئێوارەیەک

لە ڤینیز

لە ژوورێکدا

تەنیا

بێکەس

لەسەر قەرەوێڵەیەک

بێداربوومەوە

گوێم ڕاگرت

لەودیو پەنجەرەوە

دوو پیرەژن

قسەیان لەبارەی منەوە دەکرد:

"ئین کۆیله کازه چی ئوون سێنیورێ،

ما نۆن لوسسۆ کیسێ."

"ئێ ئوون ستڕانییێرۆ کێ چێر کە، لە سووه ئێنفانتسیا."

Apprivoise-moi

One afternoon
in Venice
alone
in a room
no one else
in a bed
I woke up
I heard
from the other side of the window
two old ladies
talking about me:
"In quella casa c'è un signore,
ma non lo so chi sia."
"È uno straniero che cerca la sua infanzia."

i

له
پاریس
جارجار
دەچم
لەسەر
بڵندترین
دوندی
بورجەکەی
ئیڤێل
ڕادەو هەستم؛
هەموو   شوێنێکم
لێوە   دیارە:
تەنیا   هەولێر   نەبێ!

i

in
Paris
from
time
to
time
I go
stand
at the very
top of the
Eiffel   Tower
you can   see the
whole   world:
except   Hewlêr!

شیعرێکی زۆر درێژ بۆ دایکم

غەریبیت دەکەم...

A Very Long Poem to My Mother

I miss you . . .

تەوش

من لە هەولێر، لە دایک بووم، لە بەغدا لینینم ناسی، لە تاران هەستم
بە بێ وڵاتیی خۆم کرد، لە دیمەشق بە کوردبوونم، لە ئۆسپانهۆف
چاوم کردەوە، لە ئۆلبۆرگ پەساپۆرتم وەرگرت، لە کۆپنهاگن بیری
خۆکوشتن ڕووی تێکردم، لە ستۆکهۆڵم بۆ یەکەمین جار لەگەڵ ژنێکی
ئەورووپی نوستم، لە پاریس یەکەم دیپلۆمی بێگانەم وەرگرت، لە
کراکۆف گوێم بە مۆسیقای شۆپان زاخاو درا، لە سانتیاگۆ بە ئەوین،
لە دۆسلدۆرۆف بە کینە...

ئێستا حەزدەکەم، وەک جوولەکە بازرگانە ئەمساوییەکانی سالانی
جەنگی جیهانی دووهەم، بچم ماوەیەکیش لە کەنەدا کار بکەم، پاشان
بچم ژنێک لە بەرازیل بێنم، ئینجا بێمەوە ئەورووپا و کتێبێک لە
لەندەن بڵاو بکەمەوە؛ لە کۆتاییش دا بچم لە ئەمستردام خۆم بکوژم:
لاشەکەشم، وەک فەردە پەتاتەیەکی بۆگەنکردوو فڕێبدەنە سەر
زبڵخانەیەک و هیچ کەسێکیش پێی نەزانێ.

Waste

I was born in Hewlêr, I got to know Lenin in Baghdad, I began feeling my statelessness in Tehran, my Kurdishness in Damascus, I opened my eyes in Spanov, I got my passport in Aalborg, in Copenhagen, I faced thoughts of suicide, in Stockholm, for the first time, I slept with a European woman, in Paris, I got my first foreign diploma, in Krakow, my ears were purified by the music of Chopin, in Santiago, with love, in Dusseldorf, with hatred . . .

Now I want, like the Austrian-Jewish businessmen of World War II, to go work for a while in Canada and then marry a woman in Brazil, then come back to Europe and publish a book in London, finally I will go to Amsterdam to kill myself: my corpse, like a rotting sack of potatoes, tossed into a dumpster, known to no one.

Translated by Pshtiwan Babakr and Alana Marie Levinson-LaBrosse

خەونی ئێستەتیکی

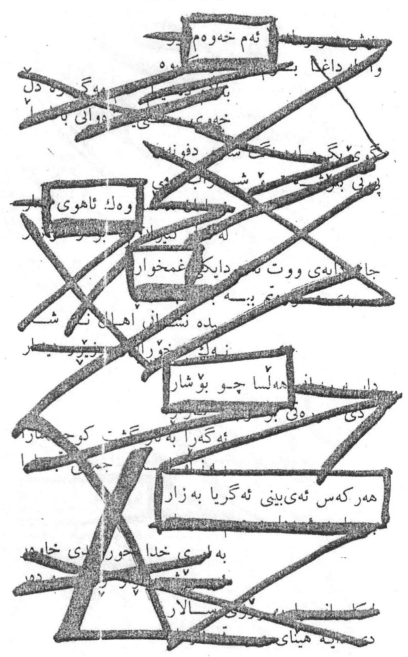

Dream Aesthetics

this dream of mine

like a deer

compassionate

got up and moved to the city

anyone who saw it wailed

شەوانی تاڵی نێو تابووتی تاریکی بیرکردنەوە لە بەدبەختییە نەتەوەییەکانی شەڕی براکوژی

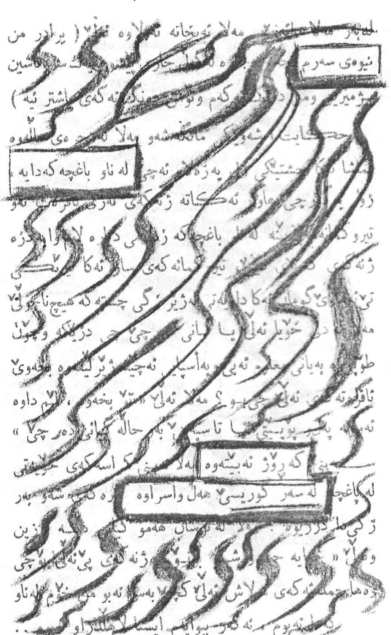

Bitter Nights inside the Dark Coffin of
Reflecting on the Hexed Patriotisms of the Fratricidal War

<u>Key:</u>
The underlying text is unidentified.

                                                 half of my head

is in the thick of the garden

                                        when day breaks

                    it is hanged from a noose

گێله پیاو

The Idiot

possessed by

a hell

full of joy and happiness

دياربەكر

Pistî temamkirina lîsê, Bedo li Stembolê kelaş di Dîcle ... Yuksek de mu ... birê ... diyo, bu ... xu ... ... nexweşxana Diyarbekirê kirine. Bedo li Diyarbekir ... kirê ... de û bavê xwe ... anîn ...

Temaşeh Hêwana mala Zîno ... nûye. Zîno hewana xwe wek a mela Be ... xwe û berd raxistiye. Li her ... ... yan dikdagnê. Li mayê ji maşê.

Sibehve bav ... û dê ... dora maşê û dil xweşî aşte dixwin.

Ser û Sekeh Zîno, fistankî nû yê bajarî de ye, kitanî ... nik û çil kirî di binguhê wê ... ye, simikak bajarî ji li nigê de ye.

Biro rîha wî kirkirî ye, şefqak li serî ..., destik kince nuh lê ye, qutkê wî ... ... qerewat e.

Bedo qutkkê sipî î zendikê ... lê ye, pantorkî paqij nikin ji li xwe kiriye.

Li ser maşê bi tepsîkî taşte raxistî ye. Zîno, çaye ji Biro ... kê. Di wî hawayê de perde vedibe.

Deyarkbekir

Key:

The underlying text comes from Musa Anter's 1959 play Birîna Reş *(Black Wound).*

Deyarbekir

cap on the head

pair of clean pants

it has worn them.

جوایەز
٢٠٠٤

Different
2004

پەناهەندەی ژمارە ٣٣٣٣٣

ئەو کاتە تەمەنم نۆزدە ساڵ بوو
هێشتا بە هەمووی نۆزدە شارم نەبینیبوو
نۆزدە گوندیش نا
نۆزدە گەڕەکیش نا
تەنانەت نۆزدە شەقامی شارەکەی خۆشم نا،
هەر بۆیەش هیچ شێعرێکم، هەرگیز، لە نۆزدە دێڕی تێپەڕ نەدەکرد.

گەنجێتیم، جەنگێک بوو؛ ڕاوی نام.
هەر زوو بیرەوەرییەکانی مندااڵیی خۆمم پێچایەوە و سەری خۆم هەڵگرت.
تاران ئەو کاتە، مزگەوتێکی گەورەی ڕەنگاوڕەنگ،
لەسەر هەر شۆستەیەکدا ژنێک: ڕەشپۆش، دانیشتبوو
بەختی گەنج و هەرزەکاری دەربەدەری وەکوو منی دەگرتەوە:
"ئاخۆ وەکوو مووسا پێغەمبەر
ئاوی ئازادی ئاوارەیی بەرەو کام مەنزڵ ڕامدەپێچی؟"

بیرم لەوە دەکردەوە بە پێ
وەک چین و ماچین تا چین بچم.
هەندێ جاریش بیرم لە کاپوول دەکردەوە،
بە خۆی و فیل و دارگوێز و گۆرانیەکانییەوە.
هەندێ جاریش دەمگوت: بچم خۆم لە ڕووباره پیرۆزەکەی سەند یان گەنج
دا هەڵبکێشم؛
بەڵکوو خواوەندەکانی ئەوی بەختێکی باشترم پێ ببەخشن.

لە ڕێگا ڕۆحی ئیبن سینا و بابەتاهیر ڕایانگرتم
لەسەر مەزارە ئاوارەکەی هەردووکیاندا چاوم بە زرخوشکی خاڵی باوکم
کەوت
کە چلوچوار ساڵ بوو، وەک خەنجەرێکی زێڕینی سەردەمی ئاشووررییەکان
لە هەولێرەوە پەڕیبووە ئەوێ:
وەک بابەتاهیر
وەک ناوی گیایەکی ناوچەی خۆشناوەتی
کە پەڕیووەتە نێو کتێبی قانون در طب ی ئیبن سینا.

116

Refugee Number 33,333

When I was nineteen years old
I hadn't even seen nineteen cities,
not even nineteen villages,
not even nineteen neighborhoods,
not even nineteen of my own city's streets,
that's why none of my poems ever exceeded nineteen lines.

My youth was a war; it chased me.
Soon I packed up my childhood memories and carried off my head.
Tehran at that time, a grand colorful mosque,
on every sidewalk, a woman: seated, all in black.
They read the fortunes of displaced youth and teenagers like me:
"Where, I wonder, will exile's sea of freedom take me, like the prophet
     Moses?"

I thought about going to China
by foot, like a guinea fowl.
And sometimes I thought about Kabul,
and its elephants, walnut trees, and songs.
And sometimes I said to myself: I should travel to the sacred Ganges or
     Sindh, and dive in
so that the gods there might give me better luck.

Along the way, the souls of Ibn Sina and Baba Tahir stopped me.
At both of their exiled graves, I met my father's uncle half sister,
who forty-four years ago, like a golden dagger from Assyrian times,
had reached there from Hewlêr:
like Baba Tahir,
like the name of a native plant from Xoşnawetî
that had reached Ibn Sina's *The Canon of Medicine*.

زرخوشکەکەی خاڵی باوکم
حەزی دەکرد کچە حەڤدە بەهارییەکەی خۆیم لێ ماره بکا،
منیش بیرم بەقوولدا چووی بیرەوەرییەکانی مندالّیی خۆم و ڕێگای ئاوارەیی
پێشم.
جمهوریت اسلامی ایران
کرج
اردوگاه پناهندگان کرد عراقی
قاوشی شەهید ئایەتوللّا مونتەزەری
پەناهەندەی ژمارە سیوسێ هەزار و سێسەد و سیوسێ
((برسد به دست فرهاد پیرباڵ))
ئەمە بوو ناونیشانی یەک ساڵی ڕەبەقی گەنجێتیی من!

لەوێدا بوو، کە من ناچار، خەونم بە ئەوروپا و ئاو و ئازادییەوە دەبینی.
لەوێ، لەناو قاوشێکی درێژی پەنجاوپێنج مەتری
کە پەنجاوپێنج قەرەوێڵەی پێنج تایی
تەنیا یەک چرای تێدا دەسووتا

لەوێ، لەناو زیندانەلانێکی وەک سەدە ناوەڕاستەکان تاریک
کە هەفتەی تەنیا حەفت سەعات دەمانتوانی چاوی هەور ببینین.
لەوێ، لەناو حەمامێک
کە سێ مانگ جارێک تەنیا یەک سابوونیان دەداینێ.
لەوێ، لەناو ئێوارەیەکی ماندووی پڕ مێشومەگەز
کە سیوسێ هەزار و سێسەد و سیوسێ کەس بە جارێک
ڕیزەمان دەگرت بۆ شەپلە گۆشتێک
یان بۆ چورکە شۆربایەکی مێشوولاویی.

لەوێ، لە تەنیشت "ساختمانی مافی مرۆڤ."
لەوێ، کە زیندانێکی ساڵانی جەنگ بوو،
لەوێ بوو کە من بۆ یەکەمین جار
خەونم بە ئەوروپا و ئاو و ئازادییەوە بینی!

My father's uncle's half sister
wanted me to marry her daughter of seventeen springs,
and I got lost in thoughts of childhood and exile's road before me.

> *Islamic Republic of Iran*
>
> *Karaj*
>
> *Refugee Camps for Iraqi Kurds*
>
> *Common Room, Shahid Ayatollah Montazeri*
>
> *Refugee number thirty-three thousand three hundred and thirty-three*
>
> *Attn: Farhad Pirbal*

This was my address for one whole year of my youth!

It was there that I was compelled to dream about Europe, water, and
   freedom.
There, in a fifty-five-meter-long common room
with fifty-five five-wheeled beds
and only one lantern lit inside it.

There, inside a small prison cell, dark as the Middle Ages,
where we could see the clouds' eyes for just seven hours a week,
there, inside a bathroom
where they gave us just one bar of soap every three months,
there, inside a tired evening filled with mosquitos
where thirty-three thousand three hundred and thirty-three people
stood in line at the same time for a palmful of meat
or a mouthful of mosquito-sullied soup.

There, next to the "Center for Human Rights."
There, a prison during the years of war,
it was there where, for the first time,
I dreamt of Europe, water, and freedom!

لەوێ،

پەیتا-پەیتا نامەی ڕۆحی دوورەوڵاتەکانمان پێدەگەیشت:

ستۆکهۆڵم تازە شەش پەناهەندەی گەڕاندبۆوە،

بەرلینی ڕۆژهەڵات هەر لە فڕۆکەخانەوە سەگی پۆلیسی بەردەداینێ،

بەرلینی ڕۆژئاوا گۆڕستانەکانی خۆی پێ پاک دەکردینەوە،

لەندەن: ناو مێترۆکانی،

فلۆرەنسا: دەیسپاردینەوە چنگ خوێناوییەکانی بەغدا

شیکاگۆ: لە برسان دەیکوشتین،

پاریس: لەسەر شۆستە نەبووایە جێگەی نەدەداینێ،

ئەو کاتەش جارێ کەسمان ناوی ئۆسلۆ و فییەنا و زیوورخی نەبیستبوو!

کۆپنهاگن بۆ من تاقە دەرگایەک بوو.

هەرچەندە دەمزانی: برا دوورەپەرێزەکەی ڕۆحم، سۆرین کیەرکیگۆرد،

سەدوسیوسێ هەزار ساڵ پێشتر

بە زەبوونی و لانەوازی لەو شارەی خۆیدا سەری نابۆوە،

گشت ئێوارەیەک کاتێ بە خۆی و گۆچانە فیدارەکەیەوە دەگەڕایەوە ماڵ

منداڵە هووڕتکەی گەڕەک بەردیان تێ دەگرت و پێیان ڕادەبوارد؛

هەرچەند دەشمزانی:

ئێین بەتووتەی مەڕاکشی

حەوت سەد و حەوت ساڵ پێشتر

چەقیبووە نێو ئەم پەنیرە ساردە بۆگەنە و نووسیبووی:

"دانمارک

کەشی بۆگەن،

زمانی بۆگەن،

ئەخلاقی بۆگەن."

بەڵام، لەگەڵ ئەوەش هەر

کۆپنهاگن، بۆ من، تاقە دەرگایەک بوو.

ئەو کاتە تەمەنم نۆزدە ساڵ بوو

هێشتا بە هەمووی نۆزدە شارم نەبینیبوو

تەنانەت نۆزدە شەقامی شارەکەی خۆشم نا.

There,

one by one we received letters from souls in faraway countries:

Stockholm had recently returned six refugees,

East Berlin police dogs mauled us at the airport,

West Berlin cleaned its graveyards with us,

London: its metros,

Florence: entrusted us to the bloody claws of Baghdad,

Chicago: starved us to death,

Paris: gave us no place but the sidewalks.

At that time, none of us had heard of Oslo, Vienna, and Zürich yet!

Copenhagen was the only door for me.

Even though I knew: my distant brother of soul, Søren Kierkegaard,

a hundred and thirty-three (thousand) years ago,

poor and displaced in his home city, put his head down

each evening when he returned home with the cane he carried for his
    epilepsy.

The neighborhood children threw stones at him, mocking him.

Even though I knew:

the Moroccan Ibn Battuta,

seven hundred and seven years ago,

had gotten stuck in this cold, rotten cheese and wrote:

"Denmark,

its weather, rotten,

its language, rotten,

its ethics, rotten."

But still,

Copenhagen was the only door for me.

At that time, I was nineteen.

I had not yet seen nineteen cities total,

من، نیوەی یەکەمی ژیانم، دوو جەنگی گەورەی ٧٤ و ٨٠ بردبوونی.
دەمویست نیوەکەی دیکەی ژیانم لە دوورەوڵاتیدا رزگار بکەم.
بە غەمگینییەوە لە خۆم دەپرسی:
"تۆ بڵێی بتوانم لەو نیوە ژیانەی دووەممەوە
وێنەی یەکەمم رزگار بکەم؟"
کاتێ تارانت بەجێ دەهێشت
کۆنترۆڵی فرۆکەخانە ڕێگەی نەدەدا پەناهەندەی کوردی عێراق
تەنانەت یەک پارچە پێنج دۆلاریشی پێ بێت!
ئی... بێ دۆلار و بەبێ پارەش لە غەریبی چی بە چی دەکرێ؟
هەندێ هەبوون لەناو نیفۆیان دەشاردەوە و دەستیشیان تا دەرباز دەبوون
لەسەر دڵیان
هەندێ هەبوون لەناو گۆرەوییان دەشاردەوە و دەستیشیان تا دەرباز
دەبوون لەسەر دڵیان
هەندێ هەبوون لەناو یەخەیان دەشاردەوە و دەستیشیان تا دەرباز دەبوون
لەسەر دڵیان
تەنانەت هەشبوون لەناو کونی قوونیان دەشاردەوە و
دەستیشیان تا دەرباز دەبوون لەسەر دڵیان.
منیش: تەنیا
چەند کتێبێک و چەند بیرەوەرییەک؛
دەستیشم تا دەرباز دەبووم لەسەر دڵم.

کە گەیشتمە ئەستەمبۆڵ دەمویست ڕۆمانێک لەسەر مەرگستانی تاران
بنووسم.
کە گەیشتمە دیمەشق دەمویست ڕۆمانێک لەسەر ئازارستانی ئەستەمبۆڵ
بنووسم.
کە گەیشتمە ئۆسپانهۆف دەمویست ڕۆمانێک لەسەر کوردستانی دیمەشق
بنووسم.

لە ئۆسپانهۆف بوو بۆ یەکەمین جار بینیم
کە من لە سەدەیەکی چەندێک کۆن و کەودەنەوە هاتووم!
چەنێک زەبوونم، چەندێک بچووک!

not even nineteen of my own city's streets.

The first half of my life was taken away from me by the two major wars of '74
and '80.

I wanted to save the other half in exile.

I sadly asked myself:

"Might I be able, with the second half of my life,

to redeem the image of my first?"

When you left Tehran

airport control didn't allow Iraqi Kurdish refugees

to carry even a single strip of a five dollar bill!

And . . . without dollars or money what can you do in exile?

Some hid it in their waistbands, with their hands stilling their hearts till they
passed through.

Some hid it in their socks, with their hands stilling their hearts till they
passed through.

Some hid it beneath their collars, with their hands stilling their hearts till
they passed through.

There were even some who hid it in their assholes,

with their hands stilling their hearts till they passed through.

And me: just

a few books and some memories;

and my hand stilling my heart till I passed through.

When I reached Istanbul, I wanted to write a novel about Deathistan in
Tehran.

When I reached Damascus, I wanted to write a novel about Painistan in
Istanbul.

When I reached Ospanov, I wanted to write a novel about Kurdistan in
Damascus.

It was in Ospanov, that I realized for the first time

that I came from such an old, foolish century!

How poor I am, how small!

له ئۆسپانهۆف بوو بینیم: وا خەریکە
نیگام بەرینتر، شیعرم دریژتر دەبیتەوە.

هەستی پڕ سویی بیولاتی و تەقەتەقی یادگارییەکان لەسەر شانم،
لەم شارەوە بۆ ئەو شار و لەم شەمەندەفەرەوە بۆ ئەو شەمەندەفەر
خۆم لە جەزیرەی میدڵ گڕاندا دۆزییەوە؛
جیهانیش، وەک سەعاتە زۆر بڵندەکەی گەرەکی جوولەکان لە شاری پراگ
بەردەوام لە پیش چاوم دەسوورایەوە و
دەم نا دەم، ئیواران
لە قولایی برینی غەریبیمدا دەزرنگایەوە.

شەش مانگ و شەش ڕۆژ لە جەزیرەی میدڵ گڕاندا مامەوە،
ئەو جەزیرەیەی هیتلەر شەش مانگ لە سەردەمی جەنگدا خۆی تیا شاردەوە
ئەو جەزیرەیەی کە لە من و شەست پەناهەندە و مریشکیکی قوندە زیاتر
هیچ زیندەوەریکی دیکەی تیدا نەدەژیا.

شار بە شار شوین پیی قورسانەکان کەوتم:
سکاگن،
ئۆلبۆرگ،
ئاغووس،
غۆسکیله،
ئینجا لە کۆتاییدا کۆپنهاگن،
کۆپنهاگن:
ئەو پەنیرە ساردە بۆگەنەی
کە دەتگوت ژنیکی مردووی گریلەندییە و بەستوویەتی!
سەیرە!
لە کۆپنهاگن بیرم دەکردەوە:
من بە حەڤدە هەزار شوین،
بە هەژدە هەزار سەعات لە زیدی خۆمەوە دوورم.
من چەند دوورم،
مندالیشم چەنیک نزیک! چ مەرگەساتیکە!

124

It was in Ospanov that I realized:
my vision is widening, my poetry is lengthening.

The longing feeling of homelessness and the memories tapping my shoulder,
from this city to the next, and from this train to the next,
I found myself on Mitte Grand Island.
And the world, like the so-tall clock in the Jewish neighborhood of Prague,
always rolled before my eyes and
from time to time, in the evenings,
it rang from the depth of my exile's wounds.

I stayed for six months and six days on Mitte Grand Island,
the island where Hitler hid for six months during the war,
an island without a single inhabitant
besides sixty refugees and one short-tailed chicken.

City by city, I followed the footsteps of the pirates:
Skagen,
Aalborg,
Aarhus,
Roskilde,
and then, at long last, Copenhagen,
Copenhagen:
that cold, rotten cheese,
like a dead old lady from Greenland, frozen solid!
How strange!
In Copenhagen I thought:
I am seventeen thousand places
and eighteen thousand hours away from my homeland.
How far away I am,
and how close my childhood! What a tragedy it is!

له کۆپنهاگن، وهک قورسانه باییره گهورهکانی خۆیان
دهبووایه ههمیشه ههر له تالان و سهفهر بم،
یانیش دهبووایه وهک بایهوان و زانا دێرینهکانی ئاووههوایان
چاوم ههر لهسهر تهرمۆمهتر
بزانم کهی پلهی گهرما کهمێک بهرزتر دهبێتهوه و خۆر دهبینم.

ئهوروپا ئهوروپایه، ئیتر
جیاوازیی گۆگادهگهی کۆپنهاگن چییه لهگهڵ گۆگادهکهی ستۆکهۆڵم؟
جیاوازیی زهردهخه درۆزنهکانی قهراغ رووباری سنێگهستین
چییه لهگهڵ زهردهخهنه ساردهخهنی قهراغ هیلسنکی؟
جیاوازیی پیاسهکانی باخی ڤیستهپۆرت
چییه لهگهڵ ههمان پیاسهکانی باخی هێدپارک؟
یان سهفهری سهر پشتی کهشتییهکی بهرهو وارشۆ
له چاو سهر پشتی کهشتییهکی بهرهو فۆلکستۆن؟
بیرهی تووبۆرگ ههمان تووبۆرگه
پهناههندهش... ههر پهناههندهیه!

بهلام لهگهڵ ههموو ئهمانهش، نهخێر:
ههر سهفهرێک وهک ناسینی کچێکی تازه وایه،
ههر سهفهرێک وهک ئهوه وایه لهگهڵ ژنێکی تردا، هیچ نهبێ چایهک
بخۆیتهوه!

پشتم کرده بهحری بهڵتیک و سهرهرۆ، لهناو چهندین شهمهندهفهری ونبوودا
وهک کۆکۆشکا لهناو تابلۆکانی خۆیدا ون بووم،
لهسهر چهندین رێگای ههڵهتهبوودا
وهک "کوڕه کهچهڵ" لهسهر رێگا ئهفسانهییهکهدا، ههڵهته بووم.
لهگهڵ چهندین زهبوونی و ئاواتدا
وهک لویجی بیراندێللۆ لهگهڵ ژنه ئیڤلیجهکهی خۆیدا، مردم.
به دوای چهندین کچه قهرهجی ههنگاری کهوتم
که لهسهر سنووره دهوڵهمهندهکانی ئهڵمانیا و سوێد
سێرکیان دهگێڕا و وهک سهرهسیڤۆن پارهیان لهناو کڵاوێکی قووۆدا کۆ
دهکردهوه.

In Copenhagen, I spent my time traveling and plundering
like their pirate great-grandfathers,
or I kept my eyes on the thermometer
like their navigators and meteorologists of old,
to see when the temperature would increase a bit so I might see the sun.

Europe is Europe, that's it.
What's the difference between Copenhagen gågader and Stockholm's?
What's the difference between the lying smiles of Snekkersten Beach
and the cold smiles of the Helsinki shoreline?
What's the difference between strolling through Vestaport Park
and the same stroll through Hyde Park?
Or the difference between a voyage on a ferry to Warsaw
and a voyage on a ferry to Folkston?
Tuborg beer is the same Tuborg
and a refugee . . . is still a refugee!

But even so, no:
each trip is like meeting a new girl,
each trip is like being with another woman, at least for a cup a tea!

I turned my back on the Baltic Sea and, reckless, among several lost trains,
like Kokoshka in his own paintings, I was lost.
On several stray roads
like "the bald boy" on his mythical road, I went astray.
With so many miseries and hopes,
like Luigi Pirandello with his paralyzed wife, I died.
I followed some Hungarian Romani girls
that pitched their circus
on the wealthy borders of Germany and Sweden
and collected coins in a hat deep as a toilet bowl.

دنیا له پێش چاوم وەک ئۆکۆردیۆنێکی ئۆسکۆتلەندی دریژتر و دریژتر
دەبوو،
چاویشم تەلی تەلەگرافی دەشتە چۆڵەکان دەییبردن،
ڕۆحیشم هەمیشه دەسپاردە ئەو باڵندە قەشەنگانەی که دەمزانی هەرگیز،
وەک ناتالی، جارێکی دیکه نایانبینمەوه.

ئاخ؛ دووره وڵاتییەکەی حاجی و ناڵی له چاو ئەوەی من: گەمەی منداڵان
بوو!

ورده ورده
وام لێ هات بۆنی هەر وڵاتێک له بۆنی وڵاتێکی دیکه
وەک ڕستەی کورتی هەمەنگوای له چاو ڕستەی دریژی پرووست
له یەکتری جودا بکەمەوه؛
وام لێ هات ڕەنگی هەر بەندەرێک له ڕەنگی بەندەرێکی دیکه
وەک چاوی پۆرترێتەکانی مۆدیلیانی له چاو چاوەکانی شاگاڵ
له یەکتری جودا بکەمەوه؛
وام لێ هات شێوەی هەر فڕۆکەخانەیەک له شێوەی فڕۆکەخانەیەکی دیکه
وەک نۆتەی غەمگینی ڤیڤاڵدی له چاو نۆتە توورەکانی ڤاگنەر
له یەکتری جودا بکەمەوه؛
وام لێ هات بۆنی ژنی هەر شارێک له بۆنی ژنی شارێکی دیکه
وەک لەشی ئافرەتەکانی گۆگان
له چاو لەشی ئافرەتەکانی جیاکۆمێتتی
له یەکتری جودا بکەمەوه.

گورگێک ئاسا که هەست به لەبەرڕۆیینی خوێنی خۆی بکا
هەستم دەکرد شیعرم
وەک تەمەنی ساغڵەم و ئاسوودەی
پیرەژنه جوولەکه پورتوگالییەکانی پاریس، ڕۆژ به ڕۆژ دریژتر دەبێتەوه.
هەستم دەکرد هەر خەتێکی که دەینووسم، دریژتر و دریژتر دەبێتەوه:
وەک ئاوارەییه ئاوییه نائومێدەکەی شەریف پاشا له مۆنتی کارلۆ...

ئەو کاته هەولێرم بەجێ هێشت، هێشتا
به هەمووی نۆزده شارم نەبینیبوو

128

Like a Scottish accordion, the world became longer and longer before my
   eyes,
and my eyes were taken by the telegraph wire across the vast plains,
and I always entrusted my soul to those beautiful birds I met, which,
like Natalie, I will never meet again.

Agh—Koyi's and Nali's exiles were child's play next to mine!

Step by step
I learned to distinguish the smell of one country
from the smell of another like
Hemingway's short sentences from Proust's long ones.
I learned to distinguish the color of one port
from the color of another like
the eyes in Modigliani's portraits from the eyes in Chagall's.
I learned to distinguish the shape of one airport
from the shape of another like
Vivaldi's sorrowful notes from Wagner's angry ones.
I learned to distinguish the scent of one city's women
from the scent of another city's like
the bodies of Gauguin's women
from the bodies of Giacometti's.

Like a wolf feeling itself bleed,
I felt my poetry.
Like the healthy, happy age
of the Jewish Portuguese ladies in Paris, it lengthened with each day.
I felt each line I wrote grow longer and longer:
        like the watery, hopeless exile of Sharif Pasha in Monte Carlo . . .

When I left Hewlêr,
I had not yet seen nineteen cities total,

تەنانەت نۆزدە شەقامی شارەکەی خۆشم نا؛
هەر بۆیەش شیعرم، هەرگیز
لە نۆزدە دێڕی تێپەڕ نەدەکرد.

پاریس: ١٩٩٢

not even nineteen of my own city's streets,
that's why none of my poems ever
exceeded nineteen lines.

Paris: 1992

سنوور

ئەلکزەندەر لەسەر پشتی من بوو، لە ئەربیل، کە داریووشی شکاند.
ئێستاش ئەوەتا، دیسانەوە، لەسەر پشتی منە کە رۆژهەڵات و رۆژئاوا تێکرا
بۆمبەکانیان بە رووی یەکتر دەتەقێننەوە:

پەپوولەم رەنگی دەپەرێت و سەردەنێتەوە
تاڤگەم، ئاوازی، کوێردەبێتەوە
بەفرم، خوێنی، ئاوارە دەکرێ.

ئاخ:
نامرۆڤایەتی بەو هەموو قورساییەی خۆیەوە لەسەر برپرەکانی پشتی لاسکە
گیام!

سەدان ساڵە وام لە نێوان دوو گۆمی شینی وان و قەزوین دا
کەچی هێشتا، هەمیشە تینووم.
سەدان ساڵە سەرم تەبای چیاکانم بەرز، کەچی هەمیشە
هەمیشە دیلم.

سەدان ساڵە لەسەر پشتی منە کە بۆرییە نەوتە پێچاوپێچەکان
فەردە برنج و قەرتاڵە روناکییەکان
بەرەو وڵاتە بەستەڵەک و دوورە دەستەکان دەگوێزرێنەوە:
خانووی خۆشم سارد
لەسەر سنوورە تاریک و تەزیوەکاندا هەر سەعاتێک
گوڵاڵەیەکی ساوای دیکەم لە برسان دەمرێ.

لەسەر خاکی نیشتیمانی خۆشمدام و لە خۆم بێگانەم.

132

Border

Alexander was on my back, in Arbela, when he defeated Darius
now, it's here again, it's on my back that the East and the West
blast their bombs in each other's faces:

my butterfly pales and dies
my waterfall, its melody, goes blind
my snow, its blood, is exiled.

Agh:
inhumanity with all its weight, on the spinal cord of my blade of grass!

For hundreds of years, there I have been between the two blue lakes of Wan
     and Qezwin
and yet, always thirsty.
For hundreds of years my head has been as high as my mountains, but
     always
always a captive.

For hundreds of years, it's happened on my back: they transport oil through
     winding pipes,
sacks of rice and baskets of glimmers
to distant, frozen countries:
and my own house, cold
on the dark, numb borders, each hour
another of my infant poppies starves to death.

I am on my homeland's soil and I am a stranger to myself.

کەرکووک، سەقز، دیاربەکر... تا قامشلی... هەمووی نیشتیمانی خۆشمە،
کەچی
لە کەرکووکەوە کە دەردەکرێم
ناتوانم بچم لە مەھاباد لە مالّە خوشکە میهرەبانەکەم بۆ ماوەیەک
بحەسێمەوە.
لە ماردینەوە کە ڕاودەنرێم
ناتوانم بچم لە ئامێدی پارچە نانێک لە مالّە برا بەخشندەکەم بخوازمەوە.

لە نێوان گۆڕی هەر برایەکم و برایەکی دیکەمدا: سنوورێک!
لە نێوان باوەشی هەر خوشکێکم و دەزگیرانەکەیدا: سنوورێک!
لە نێوان حەرفی هەر کتێبێک و کتێبێکی دیکەمدا: سنوورێک!
لە نێوان هەر ڕەنگێک و ڕەنگێکی دیکەمدا: سنوورێک!

سنوور
سنوور
سنوور
سنوور
لەسەر خاکی نیشتیمانی خۆشمدام و ئاوارەم!

١٩٩١\٤

134

Kirkuk, Seqiz, Diyarbekir . . . to Qamishli . . . all are my homeland, but
When I am expelled from Kirkuk
I can't go to Mahabad and rest for a while at my kind sister's house.
When I am chased out of Mardin
I can't go to Amedi and ask for a piece of bread at my generous brother's
    house.

Between my brother's grave and another: a border!
Between a sister's embrace of her fiancé: a border!
Between the letters of one book and mine: a border!
Between every color and one of mine: a border!

Border
border
border
border
I'm on my homeland's soil and I'm in exile!

4/1991

حکوومەتی هەرێمی کوردستان

ئێمە بخوور و مۆسیقامان لە هیندستانەوە بۆ دێت
تەلەفزیۆن و ئەجهیزەی دەقیقە لە ئیماراتەوە
برنج و ئارد لە سویسراوە
رۆشنبیری و زانست لە سووریاوە
سیاسەت و بیپسی کۆلا لە ئامریکاوە
ئەخلاق لە بەغداوە
ئایدۆلۆجیا لە یەکیەتی سۆڤیەتەوە
حیجاب لە ئێرانەوە
فیلمی خیلاعیش لە تورکیاوە
ناوی مندالەکانیشمان دەنێین: جانیه، عەلی، عەبدالقهار....

The Kurdistan Regional Government

We receive incense and music from India
television and technology from the Emirates
rice and flour from Switzerland
intellectualism and science from Syria
politics and Pepsi-Cola from America
morals from Baghdad
ideology from the Soviet Union
the hijab from Iran
pornos from Turkey
and we name our children Janiya, Ali, Abdul Qehar . . .

ئەی ڕەقیب

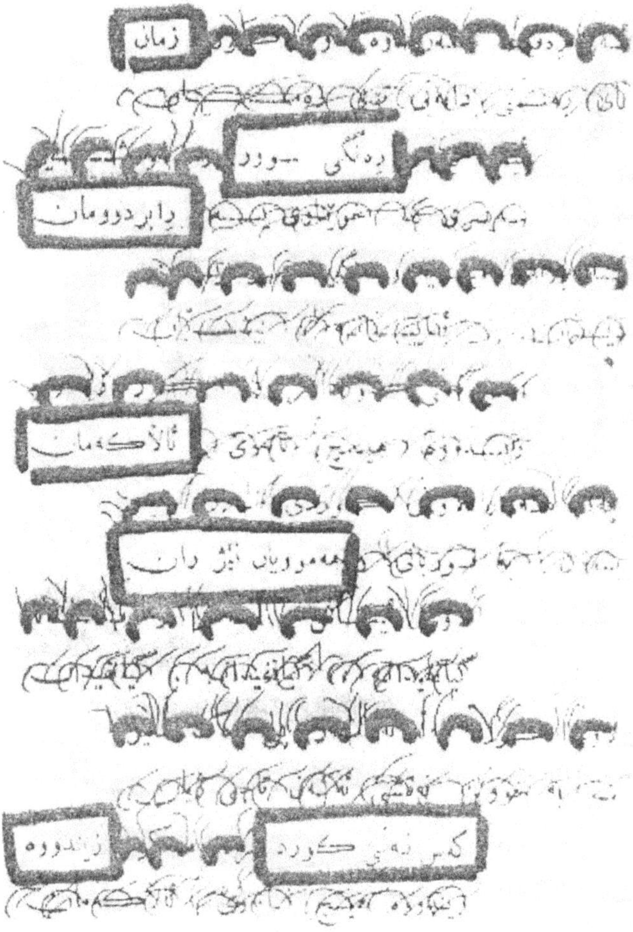

زمانی
ڕەنگی سوور
ڕاپەڕدوومان
ئالاکەمان
زیندووە
کەس نەڵێ کورد

Oh, Foe!

Key:

The underlying text is the Kurdish national anthem, written by the poet Dildar (1918–1948).

~~Oh, foe! The nation of the Kurdish~~ tongue ~~persists,~~
~~It won't be defeated by the mind's behind this era's weapons.~~

    ~~We are the offspring of~~ the color red ~~and revolution,~~
    ~~Look and see~~ our ~~bloody past.~~

~~We are the offspring of the Medes and Kay Khosrow,~~
~~Our only faith and religion is our homeland.~~

    ~~Don't say the Kurds are dead, Kurds are alive,~~
    our flag ~~is alive and bows before no one.~~

~~The youth of the Kurds are willing, and present,~~
~~willing to sacrifice, sacrifice, and sacrifice.~~

    ~~Thousands of the youth of the Kurds like roaring lions~~
    ~~Have been sacrificed, and all were buried~~

~~The youth of the Kurds stood tall like lions,~~
~~their vital crowns forged in blood.~~

    Don't say the Kurds are ~~dead, Kurds are alive,~~
    ~~our flag is alive and bows before no one.~~

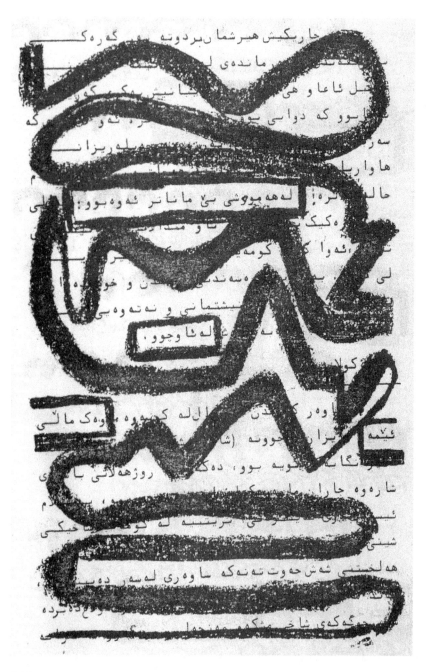

Memory of Sand

the most meaningless thing was that:

it was destroyed.

like this house
of ours

گۆرانییه ڕۆمانسییهکانی دوورهولاتی

(١)

پشتم له پیّچالا ڕۆما
قاچم له ناو ئاوه شینهکهی،
له تهنیشت سیّبهری کهنیسهیهکدا
تهماشای چهند بهلهمیّکی خهونین دهکهم.
کهمیّک ماندوو
سهرم گرانی حهشیشهی دوێنێ
چاوهڕیّ هاتنی غووزانا دهکهم:
شهش ههزار لیرهم به قهرز بداتێ.

دهمیّکی دیکه دیّت و دهیبینم:
نه ماندوویم له گیان دهمیّنێ
نه پیّویستیشم چیتر به پاره.

(٢)

له کهناری شهپۆلینی زیّی زاتهره
دهنگی کهشتیهک وهخهبهری هیّنامهوه.
برسی
ماندوو
که تهماشای کاتژمیّرم کرد:
ههژده سهعاتی ڕهبهق نوستبووم.

(٣)

له سالّی ١٤٩٢
کریستۆڤ کۆلۆمبۆس شهیدای کچیّکی هیندی ببوو.
به دووای کچه سهری ههلّگرت بهرهو هیندستان.
ڕیّی ههلّه کرد:
ئهمریکای دۆزییهوه.

142

Romantic Songs of Exile

(1)

Turning my back on Piccola Roma,
my feet in its blue water,
beside the shadow of a church,
I gaze at several dreamlike boats.
A bit tired,
my head is heavy from yesterday's hashish,
waiting for Rozana to come:
and lend me six thousand liras.

She will come in a bit and when I see her:
no tiredness will remain in my body
and I will no longer need money.

(2)

On the shore of the lapping Zatara
the sound of a ship awakened me.
Hungry,
tired,
when I checked the time:
I had been asleep for eighteen hours straight.

(3)

In the year 1492
Christopher Columbus was in love with an Indian girl.
He headed to India, chasing the girl.
He took a wrong turn:
found America.

له هاوینهههواری ئێزێڵۆ

شهقڵاوهم بیرهاتهوه:

شهقڵاوهی سهد سال دووای مهرگی خۆم.

دهلینگ کورتکردنهوهی پانتۆڵهکهم

قۆپچه

ههڵبرینگانهوه واته ئاو و ههوا خۆشبوونهوه

تهلهفۆن بۆ هاوڕێ ناونیشانی هیوای لێ وهربگرم

دارستانه چڕ و چۆڵهکهی ڤێستهپۆرت

نامهکان بدرێنم، یا بیانسووتێنم، تهنیا ئهوهی دایکم بیڵمهوه

پیڵاو. پینهدۆز. کلیلهکان

قهرزی لارس. سهلاجهکه بفرۆشمهوه ماریا

ناسنامه و کاغهزهکانم ههمووی

شهمهندهفهری ڕووهو نهڕویج له سهعات یازده و نیوی شهو بهڕێ دهکهوێ

نامه بۆ ئاراس له میوونخ

بۆ ئارام له ئهمستردام

بۆ تهها له کهنهدا

نامهیهکیش بۆ بهخه له سابلاغ، پێی بڵێم:

"چهند ڕۆژێکی تر بهیهکجاری ئێره جێ دێڵم:

جارێ نازانم بهرهو کوێ؟!"

زۆر سپێدان کاتێ له خهو بێدار دهبمهوه

یهکسهر سهرسوڕماو، چاو به دووی خۆمدا دهگێڕم، له خۆم دهپرسم:

"ئهمڕۆ له کوێم؟"

ئایا له ماڵه برادهرێکم له ستۆکهۆڵم

یان له ماڵی کچه خوشکهکهم له کارلسکۆگا؟

(4)

At a summer resort in Jesolo
I was reminded of Shaqlawa:
the Shaqlawa of a hundred years after my death.

(5)

Hem my pants
Button
Precipitation stops, meaning the weather is getting better
Call Hawre to get Hiwa's address
Vestaport's dense, empty forest
Rip up the letters, or burn them: and only keep my mother's
Shoes, shoemakers, keys
Lars's debts. Sell the refrigerator to Maria
All my IDs and documents
The train to Norway departs at eleven thirty at night
A letter to Aras in Munich
To Aram in Amsterdam
To Taha in Canada
And a letter to ol' Bachtyar in Sablagh, telling him:
"I will leave here for good in a few days:
I still don't know where to?!"

(6)

Most mornings, when I wake up,
immediately surprised, I look around, asking myself: "Where am I today?"

Am I at a friend's house in Stockholm
or at my sister's daughter's in Karlskoga?

ئایا له ماڵی کچه دۆستەکەی خۆمم له شارل میشێل
یان له قەراغێکی ڕاکشاوی گەرمەسێری شاری مارسێی؟

ئایا له ماڵی براکەمم له لووکزەمبوورگ
یان له ماڵی ئەو کچه عەرەبەی مێزۆن لیبانێز؟
ئایا لەناو فارگۆنی خەوتووی شەمەندەفەرێکم لەسەر ڕێگای
تۆرینۆ-فلۆرانس
یان له ژوورێکی تەوقیفکراوی سەر سنووری سەوزی هۆڵەندا؟

ئایا له ماڵی ئەحمەدی مەلام له بێزەنسۆن
یان له ماڵی ڕێبوار سیوەیلی له کۆپنهاگن؟

ئایا له ژووری میوانخانەیەکی پڕ پەشتەماڵم که تایبەت بۆ میوانی بەشدارانی
کۆنفرانسێک تەرخان کراوه
یان له قەراغێکی زەریای ئەتڵەنتیک که حەمباڵ و زەریاوانەکان تێیدا خەریکن
فەردەخوێ و قوتووەماسی بەرەو ئەفریقا دەگوازنەوە؟

ئایا له سالۆنی مەخمەڵیی سەر پشتی پاپۆڕێکم بەرەو وارشۆ
یان له ژوورێکی هەڵواسراوی شاری ئۆسلۆ که چاوڕێی دەرچوونی مافی
پەناهەندەییمی تێدا دەکەم؟

ئایا له ماڵی برادەرێکی حەشیشەکێش و مەیزەدەی شەوگەڕی پاریسیم
یان له متبەقی خزمەتکاری چێشتخانەیەکی پیسی شاری لیل؟
ئایا لەسەر قەنەفەیەکی شەونخوونی ئەو هۆتێلەم که شەوان پاسەوانیی تێدا
دەکەم
یان له ژووری سەرخۆشی هوتێلێکی باراناویی ئەمستردام؟

ئایا له تەنیشت ئاگردانێکی ڕاهیبەی قەیرەی فیلەندیم
یان له حەوشەی لەخەوهەڵساوی ناو وێستگەیەکی شەمەندەفەری سەر
سنووری ئیسپانیا؟

ئایا لەو ژووره شپرپێوەی ئەنتۆنی م که تەنیا بۆ دوو مانگ به کرێیان دامێ
یان له ماڵی ئەو ژنه شۆخه پورتوگاللییەی پلاس ئەرژەنتۆی
که به هەنجەتی "خۆشەویستی"
جار جار شەوانی شەممه و یەکشەممه دەمیگرته خۆی؟

146

Am I at my girlfriend's house in Saint Michel
or on the warm, reclined edge of the city of Marseille?

Am I at my brother's house in Luxemburg
or at the house of the Arab girl in Maison Libanaise?
Am I in a sleeper car on the way from Turin to Florence
or am I in a detention cell at the Netherlands' green border?

Am I at Ahmadi Mela's house in Besançon
or at Rebwar Siwaili's home in Copenhagen?

Am I in a hall decorated for a conference's special guest
or on the shore of Atlantic Ocean where the dockworkers and sailors
    transport sacks of salt and cans of fish to Africa?

Am I in a velvet suite on the back of a yacht bound for Warsaw
or I am in a teetering room in the city of Oslo, waiting to be granted my
    rights as a refugee?

Am I at a hash-smoking, night-wandering, drunkard friend's in Paris
or in the service kitchen of a dirty restaurant in Lille?
Am I on a vigilant sofa in the hotel I guard at night
or in a drunken hotel room in the rainy city of Amsterdam?

Am I next to a celibate Finnish nun's fireplace
or in the wide-awake courtyard of a train station on the border of Spain?

Am I in Anthony's messy room I was allowed to rent for just two months
or in the beautiful Portuguese lady's house on Plac Argentoi,
where for the sake of "love"
she occasionally let me in on Saturday and Sunday nights?

ئایا هێشتا هەر لەناو ئەو زەلکاوە رەشە ساردەم لە ئەورووپا
یان لە ژوورە
بەرز و ئارامە
هەردوو پەنجەرە دەم بەخەندە
جوانەکەی خۆمم؛
لە گەڕەکی تەیراوە لە هەولێر؟!

(٧)

شەقامەکانت، ئەی ئەورووپا
باخچەکانت
سەرکردەکانت
مۆزەخانەکانت
پۆلیسەکانت، کچۆڵەکانت، ژنەکانت، پەنجەرەکانت، دەرگاکانت،
مەیدانەکانت، پشیلەکانت، دووکەڵکێشەکانت، بەلەمەکانت، شەمەندەفەرەکانت،
ئوتومبیلەکانت، نافوورەکانت، فڕۆکەخانەکانت، کابینەی تەلەفونەکانت
بانقەکانت، پۆلیسخانەکانت، چیشتخانەکانت
قەراغ دەریاکانت، بانیژەکانت
سەگەکانت
پەساپۆرتەکانت
هەموو شتێکت، ئەی ئەورووپا
هەموو شتێکت بە قوربانی دارەکەی بەر ماڵمان.

(٨)

کە ئەم زۆنگاوە رەش و ساردە جێ دەهێڵم و دەگەڕێمەوە:
هەر لە یەکەم ئێوارەی گەیشتنم
تەبای مندالێکی چڵکن، گریزاوی،
خۆم لە بەردەستی دایکم شل دەکەم
تا لەناو قژی چڵکن، لوول و پێچ خواردووما کێچ
لەناو چاڵی بەقوولداچووی نێوان لامل و
شانەکانیشم: بێچووە دووپشک

Am I still in that cold black swamp in Europe
or in the high-up, quiet
room
with my two beautiful,
smiling windows,
in the neighborhood of Tairawa in Hewlêr?!

(7)

Your streets, oh Europe,
your gardens,
your leaders,
your museums,
your policemen, young girls, women, windows, doors,
squares, cats, chimneys, boats, trains,
cars, fountains, airports, telephone booths,
banks, police stations, restaurants,
sea shores, rooftops,
your dogs,
your passports
all of your things, oh Europe,
I sacrifice them all for *the tree in our front yard.*

(8)

When I leave this cold, black swamp to return home:
on the very first evening of my arrival,
like a dirty, crying child,
I will sit in my mother's lap
so she can pick
the flea from my dirty, curly, wavy hair,
the baby scorpion from the deep hollow between my neck and shoulder,

لەناو دەمی بۆگەنکردووشما: پاشماوەی کرمە ماکیاژکراوەکان

لەناو ڕۆحی تەبای کەلاوەی خاپووربووشما

لاشەی پیس و کەڕووکردووی مردووەکانم

یەک یەک بگریت و لەگەڵ دەستیا

دوور

تووڕیان هەڵیدات:

ئەو مردووانەی هەرگیزاوەهەرگیز

شایستەی ئاوڕ لێدانەوە نین.

(٩)

چوومەوە هەولێر: بۆ ئەوەی منداڵیی خۆم بدۆزمەوە.

تووشی گەنجێتیی خۆم هاتم: پیر ببوو.

the remnants of masked worms from my smelly mouth,
the filthy, moldy corpses of my dead
from my empty, ruin-friendly soul,
and fling them, one by one,
with her hands,
so very far away:
these dead that don't deserve
even a single backward glance.

(9)

I returned to Hewlêr: to find my childhood.
I bumped into my youth: it was getting old.

پارچەکانی TNT

بۆ گەڕەکی تەیراوە

بن دیواری مزگەوتێک
خۆرەتاوێک
چەند پیرەمێردێک.
پێم وابێ دوو سەد ساڵ زیاترە هەر ئەمەیە و نەگۆڕاوە.

بۆ عەزیز سەلیم

ماڵی نیگارکێشێک لە یەک ڕۆژدا چوار فەسڵە.

بۆ شەو

وەرن تەماشاکەن: ڕۆژ
چۆن بەدەست ڕازی ڕۆژگارەوە
ڕەژووی ڕازی شێتی ڕێزدەکا!

بۆ دەرۆزەکەرەکان

هیچ لەمە خۆشتر نییە لە ڤێنیز
هەموو پارەوپوولت لێ دزرابێ،
ئێوارەش بێ پەساپۆرت و بێ ناسنامە
لە کۆڵانە ئاوییەکاندا بسسوڕێتەوە...

Bits of TNT

For the neighborhood of Tairawa

At the bottom of a mosque's wall
a patch of sunshine
some old men.
I believe this is all there's been for over two hundred years, nothing has
   changed.

For 'Ezîz Selîm

A painter's house is four seasons in one day.

For the night

Come and see: how day
queues the coal of insanity's madness
in the hands of day's secret!

For beggars

Nothing is better than when, in Venice,
all your money and pennies are stolen,
and in the evenings with no passport or ID
you wander the watery alleys . . .

بۆ موسا عەنتەر

ئەم پیاوە بەستەزمانە، لەسەر سنووری عێراق – تورکیا
سەری لێ شێوابوو،
نەیدەزانی چ بکا:
دوو ملیۆن کوردی ئاوارەی برسی پێکرا بە یەک دەنگ هاواریان دەکرد:
نان...!

بۆ تەرزە فایەق جاف

زەریایەک بکە بە دۆشەگم
هەوریک بکە بە سەرینم
باخچەیەک گوڵیشم پێ دادە
با تۆ بە خەونەکانتەوە ببینم.

بۆ نەوەی دوورەوڵاتی ئەمرۆ

جەنگی عێراق و ئێران
دایکی هەموومان بوو.

بۆ ١٩٨٧

لە مانگی ساردی نۆڤەمبەردا
ئاگردانێکی بەدیاری پێشکەش کردم.

154

For Musa Anter

This poor man, at the border of Iraq-Turkey
his head confused,
didn't know what to do:
two million hungry Kurdish refugees were shouting all together in one
    voice:
Bread...!

For Terze Fayaq Jaff

Make an ocean my mattress
make a cloud my pillow
and cover me with a garden of flowers
so I can see you with your dreams.

For today's generation in exile

The Iraq-Iran war
was the mother of us all.

For 1987

In the cold month of November
it gifted me a fireplace.

بۆ سەروەر ئەحمەد

ئەم پیاوە زۆر سەیرە!
ویّرا ویّرای باخچەکە ڕۆیشت،
کەچی ئاوڕی لە هیچ گوڵیّک نەدایەوە.

بۆ ڤینیز

مەرکانی گوڵاڵەسووڕەی بەر پەنجەرەکانی، گەلیّک جوانن:
دەڵیّی عەسریّکی ڕەنگینی بەهاری شەقڵاوەیە!

بۆ دایکم

هەمین گیان، خۆزگە چاویّکت لیّم دەبوو:
لە ڕۆژی ۱۹۹۳/۸/۱۶دا،
لە شاری لۆزان، بیّ پەساپۆرت، بیّ ناسنامە، بیّ پارەوپووڵ،
دەسووڕامەوە.

بۆ عبدالرقیب یووسف

کوردستان دیّ بەیەکجاری ویّران دەکریّ:
چیا بە چیای، شار بە شاری.
هیچ کەسیّ نییە داڵدە بدا:
ئاواتی، ڕۆحی، خەونی، ئادگاری.

کوردستان دیّ بەیەکجاری لەناو دەچیّ:
گیا بە گیای، ئاش بە ئاشی.

For Serwer Eĥmed

This man is very strange!
He walked the garden end to end,
but never turned toward any flower.

For Venice

The window pots of red poppies are very beautiful:
they are like a colorful spring afternoon in Shaqlawa!

For my mother

Dear Hemin, I wish you could see me:
on the day of 8/16/1993,
in the city of Lausanne, with no passport, with no ID, no money, not a single
   penny,
I wandered.

For Abdul Raqib Yusif

Kurdistan will be destroyed entirely:
mountain by mountain, city by city.
There is no one to shelter:
its hope, its spirit, its dream, its memory.

Kurdistan will be entirely annihilated:
leaf by leaf, mill by mill.

هیچ کەسێ نییە دەنگی لێوە بێ
هیچ کەسێ نییە غەمی لێ بخوا...
−با،
ئەوەتا پیاوێک
چوار مەشقی، وەک
غەمێکی پیر
دانیشتووە
سیمای جوانی وێرانەیی دەنووسێتەوە.

بۆ پەنجەرە

ئەو کەسەی شەقامەکانی باش دیبێ
ئنجا دەزانێ پەنجەرە چییە!

بۆ شاری بێزەنسۆن

تاشەبەردەکانی قەراغ زەریا
پەڵەقەوزەی سەوزیان گرتووە،
منیش چەند پەڵە بیرەوەرییەک
لەبارەی تۆ.

بۆ چاوەڕوانی

لە فلۆرەنسە،
ڕۆژی سێ شەمووان زۆر درەنگ دێت.

There is no one to utter a word
there is no one left to grieve for it . . .
—Yes,
there is a man
sitting
legs crossed, like
an old sorrow
he is writing down the beauty-face of ruins.

For a window

Only the person has really seen the streets
will know what windows are!

For Besançon

The stones on the seashore
stained with green lichen,
and I have some stained memories
of you.

For waiting

In Florence,
Tuesdays come very late.

بۆ فەرهاد پیرباڵ

لە ئێوارەی ڕۆژی ٢٠٢٤\٥\١٥
ئاگاداری بن؛
عیزرائیل
هێواش هێواش دێ
لێی نزیک دەکەوێتەوە:
دوو پەنجەی لەسەر کونەلووتی
دوو پەنجەش لەسەر چاوەکانی
دوو پەنجەش لەسەر گوێچکەکانی؛
دەستیشی
بە هێواشی،
دەخاتە سەر دەمی و
گیانی دەردێنێ.

For Farhad Pirbal

On the evening of 5/15/2034
be aware;
Azrael
will come slowly-slowly
approaching him:
two fingers in his nostrils
and two fingers in his eyes
and two fingers in his ears;
and a hand
slowly
on his mouth
pulls out his soul.

گۆرانییەک بۆ کارڵ سەندبێرگ

من بەدرێژایی ژیانم لە هەندەران، لە خۆم دەپرسی: "ئاسوودەیی چییە؟"
من ئەم پرسیارەم لە سەدان دنیادیدەکانی دنیا پرسیوە.
من ئەم پرسیارەم لە هەموو ئەو پیاوە بەناو ساڵ کەوتووانە پرسیوە کە تێر
تێر تامی ژیانیان کردووە، هەروەها لە گەلێک مامۆستا و وەزیر و بەڕێوەبەر
و قوتابی و فەرمانبەر و تەنانەت لە جەردە و بازرگان و قاچاخچییەکانیش.
هەموویان لە وەڵامدا، ئەبلەقماو، یان وەک ئەوەی گاڵتەیان پێم هاتبێت:
بە بێباکییەوە، بە زەردەخەنەیەک، سەری نەتوانینی وەڵامدانەوەیان بۆ
ڕاتەکاندووم.

تا ئەو ڕۆژەی، کە ئێوارەیەکی چوارشەممە بوو: لە باکووری ئیسپانیا، لە
نزیک کامپۆ سانت لووکا، لەناکاو، کۆمەڵە قەرەجێکی هەنگاریم دیت، لەقەراغ
ڕووباریک، لە ژێر درەختێک دانیشتبوون، بە خۆیان و چەند بوتڵە شەرابێکی
ئاوارە و ئۆکۆردیۆنە دەنگخۆشەکانیانەوە، گۆشتیان دەبرژاند....

A Song for Carl Sandburg

Throughout my life in exile, I asked myself: "What is happiness?"
I have asked hundreds of the worldly-wise around the world.
I have asked all the aged men, those who have tasted fully-fully of life, and
also many teachers, ministers, principals, students, and employees, and I
have even asked thugs, businessmen, and smugglers. In response all of them,
bewildered, or as if they considered me as a joke: carelessly, smiling, have
shaken their heads unable to answer.

Until that day, a Wednesday evening: in the north of Spain, near Campo San
Luca, suddenly, I saw a group of Hungarian Romanis, at the edge of a river,
sitting under a tree, with some exiled bottles of wine and their nice-voiced
accordion, they were grilling meat . . .

بۆ ڕۆدانی کوڕم
۲۰۰٦

For My Son, Rodin
2006

بۆ باوکم پیرربالْ قەساب

لەگەلْ باوکم بەرِیٚ کەوتم
گەیاندمیە ژیان

لەگەلْ ژیان بەرِیٚ کەوتم
گەیاندمیە ئەوین

لەگەلْ ئەوین بەرِیٚ کەوتم
گەیاندمیە جوانی

لەگەلْ جوانی بەرِیٚ کەوتم
گەیاندمیە شیٚعر

لەگەلْ شیٚعر بەرِیٚ کەوتم؛
شیٚعر وەک خۆم سەر گەردان بوو
سەرگەردان:
نەیدەزانی رِوو بکەینە کویٚ؟

١٩٩١

For My Father, Pirbal Qesab

I walked with my father
he took me to life

I walked with life
it took me to love

I walked with love
it took me to beauty

I walked with beauty
it took me to poetry

I walked with poetry;
poetry, like me, meandered
meanderer:
it didn't know where we should head?

1991

بۆ سیگمۆند فرۆید

لەناو سەبەتەکەدا
مۆزێک
دەڵێی سولتانە
لەنێو سێوە لاسوورەکاندا.

For Sigmund Freud

In the fruit basket
a banana
sits like a Sultan
among the two-toned apples.

بۆ نەجمەدین مەلا

تۆش وەکوو من، هاوڕێم، نەجمەدین مەلا
لە ژوورەکەتدا لەناو کاغەزان
ڕۆژت لە شەو
شەوت لە ڕۆژ گرێ دەدا
بۆ ئەوەی سبەینێ حەرفێک
دەم بکاتەوە.

تۆش وەکوو من
تا سێبارەی نیوەشەوان
پاسەوانیت دەکرد بەدیار قەڵەمێکەوە
بەڵکو سبەینێ
خەونێکی خۆشی بێ
بۆ گوڵەگەنمەکان بگێڕێتەوە.

تۆش وەکوو من
ژوورەکەت هەمیشە کەشتییەک بوو
لێفت هەورێکی ڕەنگ
دۆشەکت ئازار
پەنجەرەشت ئاوازێکی ڕەنگین.
تاریکاییە بەستەزمانەکان لە دوورترین گوندەکانەوە
دەهاتنە بەردەم پەنجەرەکەی تۆ
تا گەش ببنەوە.

منیش وەک تۆ هاوڕێم، نەجمەدین مەلا
لە ژوورێکی شەش پاڵوودا
سبەینێ کە سەر دەنێمەوە
بۆ ماوەی پێنج ڕۆژ
تەنانەت فریشتەش نازانن مردووم.
ئیدی پشیله و مێروولە دێن
لە لاشەم وەردێن.

For Najmadin Mala

You, like me, my friend, Najmadin Mala,
in your room, surrounded by your papers,
knotted day to night
and night to day
so that tomorrow a letter can
open its mouth.

You, like me,
until the third midnight,
fiercely guarded a pencil
so that tomorrow
a nice dream can come
for you to recount to the florets of wheat.

You, like me,
your room was always a ship,
your duvet, the color of a cloud,
your mattress, pain,
and your window, a colorful melody.
The helpless darkness of the furthest villages
came to glitter
at your window's mouth.

And I, like you, my friend, Najmadin Mala,
in a convex room,
when I lay down my head
it will take five days
for even the angels to know that I am dead.
Then cats and ants will come
and feast on my entire body.

‒بەهەشتی چی، چاوەکەم، نەجمەدین مەلا؟
بەهەشت یەکجار دوورە.
تەنیا ئەو کەسانە دەتوانن بیگەنێ
کە ئوتومبیل یان ماتۆڕیان هەیە.

پاریس: ۱۹۹۱\۲

—What paradise, Najmadin Mala, my eyes?
Paradise is way too far away.
It can only be reached by those
who have a car or motorcycle.

Paris: 2/1991

بۆ ژەنەڕاڵ شەریف پاشا

چاوی لە پاریس
دڵی لە ژنێڤ
یار لە سلێمانی.

دایکی لە دەرسیم
باوکی لە ئەستەمبۆڵ
کچی لە ڕۆما
ژنەکەی لە قاهیرە.

خەیاڵی لای ئێمە
قەڵەمی لە لەندەن
ژوورەکەی لە ستۆکهۆڵم
پەرداخی شەرابیشی لە مۆنتیکارلۆ.

منداڵیی: لێرە
گەنجێتیی: لەوێ
گۆڕیشی تا ئێستا
هیچ کەس نازانی لەکوێیە!

For the General Sharif Pasha

His eyes in Paris
his heart in Geneva
his lover in Slemani.

His mother in Dersim
his father in Istanbul
his daughter in Rome
his wife in Cairo.

His imagination with us
his pen in London
his room in Stockholm
and his wineglass in Monte Carlo.

His childhood: here
his youth: there
and his grave even now
no one knows where it is!

بۆ دەوڵەمەندێک

سێ تاخم قەنەفە
دوو سەللاجە
پێنج تەلەفزیۆن
هەژدە پەنجەرە
دوازدە کتێب
سێ کامپیووتەر
سێ پلەی ستێیشن (کە یەکێکیان شکاوە)
دوو موەلیدە
حەوت پەساپۆرت
پێنج جنسیەی عێراقی (یەکێکیان تەزویرە)
سی و شەش پەردە (دوازدەیان لە ماڵەوە کەوتوون)
بیست و دوو کورسی، شەش مێز
چوار بوتڵ غاز (کە یەکێکیان هەمیشە بۆشە)
نۆ سۆبە، هەشت سپلێت، چوار هیتەر
هەزار و پێنج سەد وێنە
نۆزدە ئەلبووم
یەک جۆللانە
سێ حەمام (یەکێکیان خاریجی)
سێ ئۆتۆمبیل، پازدە دەرگا، حەفدە ئاوێنەی دیوار، نۆ ئاوێنەی بچووکی
دەستی، سێ ئاوێنەی سەرمێز، پێنج کانتۆری جلوبەرگ، چوار ئوتوو (کە
دوویان ئیش ناکا)، دوو غەساڵە، یەک ئامێری شۆردنی قاپ، سێنزە تەپڵەکی
جگەرە، سێ مەعرەزی شووشەوات، یەک باخچەی گەورە، دوو کەرویشک،
سەد چۆلەکە، یەک مشک، نۆ پشیلە، یازدە زبڵدان (دووی گەورە و نۆی
بچووک)، سێ چەکمەجە، هەژدە قات سەترەوپانتۆڕ، پەنجا و سێ کراس،
نۆزدە دەرپێی قوتە، دوو سیفۆن، هەشت لیفکە، چوار موبەریدە، سێ پانکە،
یەک سەماوەر، پازدە مۆمدان، سی و شەش مۆم، یازدە سندووق بیپسی،
نۆ عەلاگە، یەک دەمانچە، سێ کلاشنکۆف، بیست قەڵەمی ماجیک، دوو
قەڵەمدان، دوو سەد و پەنجا سیدی، هەشتا و پێنج کاسێتی ڤیدیۆ، سێ
تەسجیل، بیست و هەشت ئامێری ژمێریاری (کە دەیان ئیش

For the Rich

three sets of sofas

two refrigerators

five televisions

eighteen windows

twelve books

three computers

three Playstations (one of which is broken)

two generators

seven passports

five Iraqi residency cards (one of which is fake)

thirty-six curtains (twelve on the floor of the house)

twenty-two chairs, six tables

four tanks of propane (one of which is always empty)

nine oil stoves, eight air conditioners, four space heaters

one thousand five hundred pictures

nineteen albums

one porch swing

three bathrooms (one of which is outdoors)

three automobiles, fifteen doors, seventeen wall mirrors, nine small hand
mirrors, three dresser mirrors, five wardrobes, four irons (two of which do
not work), two washing machines, a dishwasher, thirteen ashtrays, three
display cabinets, one big garden, two rabbits, a hundred sparrows, one
mouse, nine cats, eleven trash cans (two of which are big and nine of which
are small), three chests of drawers, eighteen suits, fifty-three shirts, nineteen
pairs of panties, two toilets, eight washcloths, four desert coolers, three fans,
one samovar, fifteen candlesticks, thirty-six candles, eleven plastic cases for
Pepsi bottles, nine plastic bags, one handgun, three Kalashnikovs, twenty
markers, two pencil sharpeners, two hundred and fifty CDs, eighty-five
video cassettes, three voice recorders, twenty-eight calculators (ten of which

ناكا)، دوو ڤیدیۆ، چوار عەینەک، نۆ تەسبیح، نۆزده جووت پێڵاو، هەشتا و
پێنج جانتای ژنانەی دەستیی
سێ سەتەلایت
هەژده مەمکدان
نۆ ئەتەگ
پەنجا کراس
یازده مافوور (سێی کاشانه)
بیست بوتڵ بیره
یازده بوتڵ ویسکی
سی و حەفت گڵۆپ
نۆزده جەنتای گەورەی سەفەری
چوار تانکی ئاو
پێنج بەرمیل نەوت (دووانی هەمیشه بەتاڵن)
یەک پاسکیلی ٢٨
سێ پاسکیلی ٢٤
سێ قەڵەم
شەش دەفتەر
سی و شەش تابلۆی له چوارچێوەی گیراوی هەڵواسراوی دیوار
چوار سەعاتی چاڵمه، دوو سیسەمی دوو نەفەری، هەشت سیسەمی یەک
نەفەری،
پازده مەنجەڵ، چوارده شانه، سی و شەش مەتر سۆنده، هەشتا فەخفووری،
هەشت خوێدان،
دوو شەکردان، سێ قۆریه
دوو کتلی...
لەگەڵ
ملیۆنێک سەریەشه و مەژغەڵەت و خەم و خەفەت
بەبێ هیچ شادی و ئارامی و
تەنانەت تۆزقاڵێکیش چییه
ئاسوودەیی.

do not work), two VCRs, four eyeglasses, nine prayer beads, nineteen pairs
of shoes, eighty-five women's purses
three satellites
eighteen bras
nine pairs of pajamas
fifty dresses
eleven rugs (three of which are from Kashan)
twenty bottles of beer
eleven bottles of whiskey
thirty-seven lightbulbs
nineteen large suitcases
four water tanks
five oil barrels (two of which are always empty)
one 28-inch bicycle
three 24-inch bicycles
three pencils
six notebooks
thirty-six framed, hanging paintings
four grandfather clocks, two king-size beds, eight twins, fifteen pots, four-
teen combs, thirty-six meters of hose, eighty porcelain dishes, eight saltshak-
ers, two sugar pourers, three teapots
two kettles . . .
with
a million headaches, banalities, and sadnesses
no happiness or peace
not even a single grain of
comfort.

بۆ ئێرنست ڕۆدان

ڕووت و قووت، لەسەر چیچکان، نوقمی تەئەممول
پەنجەکانی لەژێر چەنە دانیشتووه و بیر دەکاتەوه.

ڕووت و قووت دانیشتووه و بیردەکاتەوه.
ئێمەش هەموومان کۆکپۆش
به کەوا و سەڵتەوه، به سەتره و پانتۆڵەوه، به جبه و عەباوه
(هەریەکەی بەجلوبەرگی وڵاتەکەی خۆیەوه که له مندالیەوه پێی ڕاهاتووه).
به تەنیشتیدا تێدەپەڕین
هەر یەکەمان تەنیا جارێک
(چونکه ئێمه لەسەر زەوی ڕێبوارێکین زوو گوزەر).
به تەنیشتیدا تێدەپەڕین و تەماشای دەکەین
هەندێکمان خەفەتناک، هەندێکمان دڵشاد
هەندێکمان به گاڵتەجاڕیەوه
هەندێکیشمان سەرسوڕماو:
"ئەم پیاوه بۆچی ڕووت و قووت دانیشتووه و بیردەکاتەوه؟"
"ئەم پیاوه له کەیەوه
هەر لێره ڕووت و قووت دانیشتووه و بیر دەکاتەوه؟"
"ئەم پیاوه ئاخۆ تاکو کەی
تاکو کەی ڕووت و قووت دەمێنێتەوه و... هەر بیردەکاتەوه؟
...تا کەی؟!"

180

For Ernst Rodin

Naked, perched, sunken in contemplation,
the fingers of one hand beneath his chin, seated, he thinks.

Naked, seated, he thinks.
And all of us are well dressed
in kewa and salta, in our outfits, in our jubba and abaya
(each in our traditional clothes, which we have worn since childhood).
We pass him by,
just once each
(because here on earth we are travelers passing swiftly by).
We pass by and gaze at him,
some of us sad, some of us happy hearted,
some of us jokingly,
and some of us awed:

     "Why is this man sitting naked, thinking?"
     "How long has this man
     been sitting right here, thinking?"
     "This man, I wonder, how long,
     how long will he sit naked . . . thinking?
     . . . how long?!"

بۆ خۆشەویستێکم

منداڵ نان دەخوا دایک پێی دڵخۆش دەبێ.
من شیعر دەنووسم تۆ زەردەخەنە دەتگرێ.
تۆ پێدەکەنی... من شیعرێک دەنووسم.

For a Lover of Mine

The child eats and the mother is happy.
I write poems, you smile.
You laugh . . . I write a poem.

بۆ حوسێن حوزنی موکریانی

ئەی مام و مامۆستای مەزنم، موکریانی!
من، ڕاستییەکەی، زۆر دەترسم ئەگەر بمرم
وەک تۆ پەیکەرم بۆ دروست بکەن:
چونکە دەبینم
لە مەیدانی بەردەم قوتابخانەیەکی بێ ئاودەسخانە لە ڕواندز
پەیکەرێکیان بۆ تۆ
لە مەیدانەکەی پارێزگای هەولێریش
پەیکەرێکیان بۆ برا بچووکەکەت گیوی دروست کردووە:
خۆت و براکەت
کە بۆ ماوەی پەنجا و پێنج ساڵ هەر یەکەتان
ئازاد، جەربەزە، گەرۆک بەسەر پشتی باوە
شەیدای سەفەر و گەنجینەکان
نەتاندەویست زیندانکراوی هیچ وڵات و ڕۆتینێک بن.
کەچی ئەمرۆ
ئەو لە هەولێر و تۆ لە ڕواندز
بازرگانیتان پێوە دەکەن؛ لەمەش خراپتر
هەردووکتان حەپسی ئینفرادیی
ناو زنجیرێکی پیس ڕەش
لەناو چێورمەیەک.
باڵندە جیقنەتان بەسەردا دەکەن
سەگی ئێوارانیش پێتان دەحەڕن.
هەر باش بوو زیندووش نەبوون ئەمرۆ
ئەگینا لەم بێ کارەبایی و قات و قڕییەدا
بە ئەنفلۆزایەکی عەنتیکەشەوە دەمردن.

For Hussein Huzni Mukryani

Ah, my uncle and great teacher, Mukryani!
To be honest, I am quite afraid that if I die
they will make a statue of me like you:
because I see
on the square in front of a school with no bathrooms in Rwanduz
they made a statue of you
and another of your little brother Giwi
on the square in front of the Hewlêr Governorate hall:
you and your brother,
for about fifty-five years each—
free, fearless, wanderers on the wind's back,
fond of traveling and treasures—
sought not to be imprisoned by any nation or routine.
But today,
he in Hewlêr and you in Rwanduz,
they have sold you out; and worse still,
you're both in solitary, confined
by a dirty chain   black
beneath a gravestone.
The birds are shitting on you
and the dogs bark at you at dusk.
It is good that you are not alive today.
Otherwise you would have died
from this famine and lack of electricity,
from a strange strain of the flu.

بۆ ژادانۆف

ئوتومبیلێکی هەیئەتی ئیداری و کۆبوونەوەیەکی علوج
قوتابییەکی دەستی دووەم و تەلەفزیۆنێکی تەمبەڵ
تەسبیحێکی ملیۆنێر و بازرگانێک کە لە حەجەوە هاتووە
کچێکی پڕ و زبڵدانێکی بێ وەفا
سەفەرێکی کورت و پانتۆڕێکی جەماعی
مە نجەڵێکی تەقاویت و بێوەژنێک ئاوی کوڵاو
حەمامچییەکی دووکەڵاوی و چایخانەیەکی خەواڵوو
چۆلەکەیەکی قورس و دەرسێک کە لاقی شکاوە
هەکەمێکی گەردەن کەش و شاخێکی کورتەبالا
پرتەپرتی خە ڵک و پەرلەمانی بێوەژنان

گۆرانیبێژێکی ٢٨ و پاسکلێکی دەنگخۆش
ئاگرێکی سە رخۆش و نووسەرێکی بلێسەدار
موەلیدەیەکی زانکۆ و خوێنکارێکی شکاو
تاڤگەیەکی تەقاویت و پێشمەرگەیەکی بەقەلبەز
جودابوونەوەیەکی بێ عەقڵ و رۆشنبیرێکی بێ هات و هاوار

نەجارێکی تاڵ و چایەکی دە سترەنگین
حاکمێکی تەنگ و پێڵاوێکی دادپەروەر
کۆمپیووتە رێکی دوور و گوندێکی پەنتیۆم چوار
کراسێکی سێ نهۆم و باڵەخانەیەکی ئاودامان سوور
زانکۆیەکی پڕ لە تاسە و جادەیەکی پڕ مەعریفەت

گۆڵێک بەرووتی و ژنێک بەپەنەرتی
کۆرێکی بەحەپەحەپ و سەگێکی بەسوود
ئەسپێکی شارەزا و مامۆستایەکی چەمووش
پەناهەندەیەکی قووڵ و زەریایەکی بێ پەساپۆرت
مەلایەکی توندوتیژ و خۆپیشاندانێکی قورئانخوێن
وەزیرێک پێنج ماکەری لە ماڵەوە بەستۆتەوە و
ئاشەوانێک پێنج ژن لە ماڵەوە بەخێو دەکا

For Zhdanov

an administrative board car and a stolen meeting
a secondhand student and a lazy television
a millionaire tasbih and a businessman returning from hajj
a full girl and a disloyal trash can
a short trip and group pants
a retired pot and a widow of boiled water
a smoky bath-keeper and a sleeping chaixana
a hard sparrow and a lesson with a broken leg
an unyielding referee and a short mountain
a people's grumbling and a widows' parliament

a 28-inch singer and a bicycle with a nice voice
a drunk fire and a blazing writer
a university generator and a broken student
a retired waterfall and a splashing peshmerga
a stupid separation and a quiet intellectual

a bitter carpenter and a handy tea
a tight judge and a just shoe
a faraway computer and a Pentium 4 village
a three-story dress and a red-hemmed building
a university full of speed bumps and a street full of knowledge

a naked goal and a penalty woman
a barking gathering and a useful dog
an experienced horse and a crazy teacher
a deep refugee and an ocean with no passport
a violent mullah and a Qu'ran-reading protest
a minister ties up five mares at home and
a miller feeds five women at home

شوڕتی مرووریکی کراوه و پەنجەرەیەکی زیرەک
ژنێکی بێ سەنەوی و ئوتومبیلێکی چاوبەکل
مامۆستایەک کە لە ڕۆژێکدا سێ جار دەکوژێتەوه و
کارەبایەک کە سلفەی زەواجی بۆ کراوه و چۆتە شەهرالعسل
فڕۆکەخانەیەکی بەقەوچەقەوچ و پڕۆفیسۆرێکی پاک و تەمیز
دارچنارێکی بێ ئامان و تێکگیرانێکی ناو مەحکەمە
لەگەڵ
پەرلەمانتارێکی کۆنەجاش و ڕەفیق حیزبییەکانی نیشتیمانپەروەر

وەزیرێکی کۆنە بەعسی و نائیب عەریفێکی ڕۆشنبیر
سەرۆک زانکۆیەکی گەوج و
خێرخەبەرێکی پسپۆڕ لە ئەوروپا گەڕاوەتەوه
مودیرێک دەستی بەخوێنی ئەنفال سوور و
کڵاشنکۆف لە شانێکی دەسپاک
لەگەڵ
کوردستانێکی ژێردەست و عێراقێکی ئازاد!

ئەمەیە واقیعییەتی شۆڕشگێڕی ئێمە،
ئەی دوژمنی سەرسەختی سوریالیزم و عەبەسییەت و دادایزم...
جەنابی ژدانۆف!

an open traffic cop and a smart window

a woman with no registration and an automobile with kohled eyes

a teacher that turns off three times a day and

a power source that takes out a starter loan and goes on a honeymoon

a blathering airport and a clean professor

an unsafe sycamore and a quarrel at the courthouse

and

a jackass parliamentarian and a patriotic party membership

a former Ba'athist minister and an intellectual deputy corporal

a stupid university president and

a good-news expert returned from Europe

an administrator whose hands are red with Anfal's blood and

a Kalashnikov carrier whose hands are clean

and

a seized Kurdistan and a free Iraq!

This is the reality of our revolution,

you, stubborn enemy of Surrealism, Absurdism, and Dadaism . . .

Esteemed Zhdanov!

بۆ شێخ مەحموود

لە زەمانی تۆدا گەنجی کورد
بۆ یەکەمین جار لە مێژووی چەوساندنەوەی خۆیدا
توانی بزانی بوێری دەم بکاتەوە و
بە ڕابردووی بێ عەقڵ و ئەمرۆی بێ ئەخلاق بڵێ: نا.

لە زەمانی تۆدا لاوی کورد
بۆ یەکەمین جار لە مێژووی کۆیلەیی خۆیدا
لە گەرمەی خەوی پڕ پرخەپرخی پیر و پۆلیس و مەلا و شێخان
زانی بتوانی بوێری
چاو بکاتەوە و "خەونێک" ببینی.

لە سەردەمی تۆدا خوێندکاری کورد
بۆ یەکەمین جار لە مێژووی لاقە و فەلاقە و حەیزەراندا
توانی بوێری بزانی زنجیری عەقڵی بکاتەوە و
بە گڕ پیرە پەتیارە و پەککەوتووەکاندا بچێتەوە.[1]

١. بەڵام حەیف، تۆ؛ ئەی پایەدار
لەجیاتی پشتیوانی لێکردنمان؛ هاتیت
زاڵم زاڵم
پشتی نەفرەتت لەو گەنجە کرد کە خەونەکەی دیت؛
گەنجەکەی دیکەشت – کە توانیبووی بوێری
زنجیری عەقڵی بکاتەوە –
لەناو خوێنی خۆیدا گەوزاند.

190

For Sheikh Mahmud

In your time,
for the first time in their oppressed history,
young Kurds could dare, aware, to open their mouths and
say to the stupid past and immoral present: *no.*

In your time,
for the first time in their enslaved history,
in the snoring depths of their elders, police, mullahs, and sheikhs' sleep,
young Kurds could dare, aware,
to open their eyes and "dream."

In your time,
for the first time in their history of being raped, kicked, and caned,
Kurdish students could dare, aware, to unzip their brains
and stand up to their obstinate, impotent elders.[1]

---

1. But alas, you, oh steadfast one,
rather than supporting us, you came and—
oppressor oppressor—
turned your fucking back on the youth who dreamt.
And the other youth—who dared
unzip their brains—
you drenched them in their blood.

بۆ ئەحمەدی مەلا

ڕۆژێکیان
بۆ نووسینی شیعرێک
پێویستیم بە مشتێ ڕەنگی شین هەبوو.
چوومە لای ئەحمەدی مەلا.
داوای مشتێ ڕەنگی شینم لێی کرد، وتی:
"بەداخەوە ڕەنگی شینم نەماوە.
هانی پارچەیەک خەیاڵت بدەمێ.
بۆ خۆت بیکە بە ڕەنگی شین!"

ڕۆژێکیان ئەحمەدی مەلا
بۆ نووسینی شیعرێکی خۆی
پێویستی بە مشتێ ئاواز هەبوو.
هات داوای مشتێ ئاوازی لێم کرد، وتم:
"بەداخەوە ئاوازم نەماوە.
هانی پارچەیەک هەستی بێ وڵاتیی خۆمت بدەمێ.
بۆ خۆت بیکەرە ئاواز!"

١٩٩١/١٢/٨

192

For Ahmadi Mela

One day
I needed a handful of the color blue
to write a poem.
I went to Ahmadi Mela.
I asked for a handful of the color blue, and he said:
"Unfortunately, I no longer have the color blue.
But here you go—I can give you a bit of imagination.
Turn it into blue yourself!"

One day Ahmadi Mela
needed a handful of melody
to write a poem of his own.
He came to ask for a handful of melody, and I said:
"Unfortunately, I no longer have any melody.
But here you go—I can give you a bit of the feeling of statelessness.
Turn it into a melody yourself!"

8/12/1991

بۆ فیۆدۆر داستایۆڤیسکی

ئوستادی گەورەم، دستۆڤسکی!
زۆر سەیرە
ئەوانەی تۆ دەخوێننەوە، هەر دەبێ گۆڕانێکیان بەسەردا بێت:

ئەوەی بێ ئیمانە، ئیمانی لەلا دروست دەکەی
ئەوەی ئیماندارە، ئیمانی نامێنێ

ئەوەی ترسنۆکە، ئازای دەکەی
ئەوەی ئازایە، ترسنۆکی دەکەی

ئەوەی بێ شەرمە، شەرمنی دەکەی
ئەوەی شەرمنە، بێ حەیای دەکەی

ئەوەی پوولدارە
وای لێدەکەی هەموو پارەی خۆی بداتە هەژارەکان
ئەوەی بێ پارە و پوولە
وای لێدەکەی هەرچی بکات حەلاڵ بێ لە پێناو پارە

ئەوەی دەیەوێ خۆی بکوژێ
پەشیمانی دەکەیتەوە و هیوای ژیانی پێ دەبەخشی
ئەوەی گەشبینە و دڵی بە دنیا خۆشە
وای لێ دەکەی خۆی بکوژێ

ئەوەی سۆزانییە، دەکەیتە فریشتە
ئەوەی فریشتەیە، دێ سووک سووک لەشی خۆی دەفرۆشێ
ئەوەی گێلە، هۆشیاری دەکەیتەوە
ئەوەی هۆشیاریشە، "گێل" دەبێ

For Fyodor Dostoevsky

My great master, Dostoevsky!
It's so strange
Those who read you are changed:

Those who are faithless, you give faith
Those who are faithful, you turn toward faithlessness

Those who are cowards, you make strong
Those who are strong, you make cowards

Those who are shameless, you make shy
Those who are shy, you make shameless

Those who have money
You make give it all to the poor
Those who have no money or means
You make anything they do for money halal

Those who want to kill themselves
You talk out of it and give hope for life
And those who are optimistic and happy-hearted about this world
You make kill themselves

Those who are prostitutes, you turn into angels
And those who are angels begin bit by bit to sell their bodies
Those who are idiots, you awaken
And those who are awakened become idiots

ئەوەی قوماڕچییە، واز لە قومار دەهێنێ
ئەوەی تەنانەت هیچ شتێکیش لە قومار نازانێ
دەیکەیتە پیسترین قوماربا

ئەوەی خوا لە دڵیایەتی، دەبێتە شەیتان
ئەوەی شەیتان لە دڵیایەتی، دەبێتە قەددیس

ئەوەی ناتناسێ دەتناسێ
ئەوەی دەتناسێ، تاهەتایە سڵت لێ دەکاتەوە

زۆر سەیرە، ئوستادی گەورەم، دەستۆفسکی!
من، هەرگیز ناوێرم جارێکی دیکە لە تۆ نزیک بکەومەوە.

Those who are gamblers give up gambling
And those who know nothing about gambling
You make the dirtiest gamblers

Those who have God in their heart become devils
Those who have Satan in their heart become saints

Those who don't know you, know you
Those who know you will be afraid of you forever

It is strange, my great master, Dostoevsky!
I can't draw near you again.

بۆ پەیمان بەگۆگ

لە کاتژمێر هەشتی بەیانییەوە تا دووی پاش نیوەڕۆ
وابزانم لە کارگەیەکی پێڵاو دروستکردن کاردەکات لە کۆپنهاگن.
لە کاتژمێر دووی پاش نیوەڕۆشەوە تاکو پێنجی ئێوارە
لەناو بار و شەقام و قاوەخانەکاندا دەسووڕێتەوە.
لە پێنجی ئێوارەشەوە تا هەشتی شەو
لەگەڵ کچە ئێرلەندی و ئێرانی و جوولەکە پۆڵەندییەکان
لە شەوبێرییەکاندا
هەر دەیەوێت و هەوڵ دەدا
هەستی دوورەوڵاتیی خۆی بڕەوێنێتەوە.

لە هەشتی شەوییشەوە تا یازدەی شەو
لە ماڵی بێوەژنێکی سریلانکی
دادەنیشێت و
هەر دەیەوێت و هەوڵدەدا
هەستی دوورەوڵاتیی خۆی بڕەوێنێتەوە.

لە یازدەی شەوییشەوە
دەگەڕێتەوە ماڵ.
دەست دەداتە ڕۆمانێکی ئەندرسن و
هەر دەیەوێت و هەوڵ دەدا
هەستی دوورەوڵاتیی خۆی بڕەوێنێتەوە.

لە یازدە و دووازدە دەقیقەی شەوییشەوە
وردە وردە و
پاشان لەناکاو
دەست بە کتێبێکەوە
خەوی لێ دەکەوێ:
لە خەویدا گەڕاوەتەوە هەولێر.
منداڵێکە و لە گەڕەکی ناو قەسران.
لەودیو دیوارە بڵندەکەی ماڵی چەلەبی
خەریکە پرتەقاڵ بەدزییەوە لێ دەکاتەوە.

For Peyman Begog

From eight o'clock in the morning until two in the afternoon
I believe he works in a shoe factory in Copenhagen.
And from two in the afternoon until five in the evening
he wanders the bars, streets, and coffee shops.
And from five in the evening until eight at night
with the Irish, the Iranians, and the Jews from Poland
in the brothel
he desires and attempts
to release his feelings of exile.

And from eight until eleven at night
he sits in the house of a widowed Sinhalese woman and
he desires and attempts
to release his feelings of exile.

And at eleven at night
he returns home.
He reaches for one of Anderson's novels and
he desires and attempts
to release his feelings of exile.

From eleven or twelve at night
little by little
and then suddenly
book in hand
he falls asleep:
in his dreams he has returned to Hewlêr.
He is a child in the neighborhood of Naw Qesran.
Behind the high wall around Chalabi's house
he's stealing oranges from the tree.

بۆ هاشم سەراج

بابەتاهیری هەمەدانی شیعرێکی جوانی نووسی و
بۆ مەلای جەزیری خوێندەوە
ئەویش چوو بۆ نیزامی گەنجەویی خوێندەوە
ئەویش هات بۆ خانای قوبادیی خوێندەوە
خانای قوبادی چوو بۆ المتنبی ی خوێندەوە
ئەویش چوو بۆ مەحویی خوێندەوە
ئەویش چوو بۆ مەولەویی خوێندەوە
مەولەویش هات بۆ شێخ رەزای خوێندەوە
ئەویش چوو بۆ بۆدلێری خوێندەوە
ئەویش چوو بۆ ت.س. ئێلیۆتی خوێندەوە
ئێلیۆتیش هات بۆ بەدر شاکر سەیابی خوێندەوە
ئەویش هات بۆ عەبدوللا گۆرانی خوێندەوە
ئەویش چوو بۆ عەبدوللا پەشێوی خوێندەوە
پەشێویش هات بۆ خزعل الماجدی خوێندەوە
ئەویش هات بۆ جەمال غەمباری خوێندەوە
ئەویش چوو بۆ دڵشاد عەبدوللای خوێندەوە
دڵشاد عەبدوللاش هات بۆ کەریم دەشتیی خوێندەوە
ئەویش چوو بۆ ئازاد دڵزاری خوێندەوە
ئەویش چوو بۆ هاشم سەراجی خوێندەوە
هاشم سەراجیش هات بۆ منی خوێندەوە
منیش ئەمەتا
شیعرەکەم بۆ ئێوە خوێندەوە.

For Haşm Serac

Baba Tahir Hamadani wrote a beautiful poem and
read it to Malaye Jaziri
who went to read it to Nizami Ganjavi
who came to read it to Khana Qubadi
and Khana Qubadi went to read it to Al-Mutanabbi
who went to read it to Mahwi
who went to read it to Mawlawi
and Mawlawi came to read it to Sheikh Raza
who went to read it to Baudelaire
who went to read it to T. S. Eliot
and Eliot came to read it to Badr Shakir Al-Sayyab
who came to read it to Abdulla Goran
who went to read it to Abdulla Pashew
and Pashew came to read it to Khazal Almajidi
who came to read it to Jamal Ghambar
who went to read it to Dilshad Abdulla
and Dilshad Abdulla came to read it to Karim Dashti
who went to read it to Azad Dilzar
who went to read it to Haşm Serac
and Haşm Serac came to read it to me
and here I am
reading the poem to you.

بۆ ئێرنست ھەمەنگوای

ھەمەنگوای عەینەن لە جەنگی جیھانیی دووەم دەچێ:
پڕ لە ھەرا، گوللە، خوێن، ڕاکردن، ئیسعاف،
شەمەندەفەری وەرگەڕاو، ڕەشماڵی بریندار،
جێبی لە قوڕ چەقیو،
پرسە، مردن، یەکتر جێھێشتن، ئاویلکەیی و ھاتوھاواری کوژران...
کەچی ھەمیشە لێوانلێوە
لە عەشق و جوانی و ڕاز و نیاز و سۆز و عەتر و ئاواز و
زەردەخەنە و
ئومێد.

For Ernest Hemingway

Hemingway is just like the Second World War:
full of noise, bullets, blood, running, ambulances,
upturned trains, field hospitals,
mired Jeeps,
funerals, death, departure, last breaths, and murderous screams . . .
But always full to the brim
with love and beauty and secrets and wishes and affection and perfume and
 melody and
smiles and
hope.

بۆ کچەکانی قسمی داخلی

کارەبا:... سفر

یەک دەرگا

یەک پەنجەرە

یەک مجەفیفە

یەک کانتۆری جلوبەرگ

یەک رادیۆ (ئەویش شکاو)

یەک موبەریدە

یەک موسەجیلە

دوو سیسەم

سێ خەم و خەفەت

چوار دیوار

لەناو چوار دیوار

پێنج شەممەیە و

هەزاران راز و نیاز.

For the Girls at the Dormitory

electricity: . . . zero
one door
one window
one hairdryer
one wardrobe
one radio (which is broken)
one desert cooler
one voice recorder
two beds
three sorrows
four walls
within the four walls
it is Thursday and
there are thousands of secrets and wishes.

بۆ بێرنارد کووشنەر

ئەگەر باخچەی ماڵێکت بینی و پیس بوو
مانای وایە ژن و مێردەکە میانەیان لەگەڵ یەکتر تەواو نییە.

ئەگەر شەقامێکت بینی پیس بوو
مانای وایە میللەت و حکوومەت
میانەیان لەگەڵ یەکتر تەواو نییە.

ئەگەر شۆستەیەکت بینی خوێنی ئینسانی لەسەر ڕژابوو
مانای وایە
هەموو مرۆڤایەتی دەیەوێ کۆتایی بەیەکتر بێنێ.

For Bernard Kushner

If you see a house with a dirty garden
it means the husband and wife are not getting along.

If you see a dirty street
it means the people and the government
are not getting along.

If you see the sidewalk wet with blood
it means
each side of humanity wants to end the other.

بۆ هێمن

شاعیرێک هەبوو
لە شارێک دەژیا
کە چل و شەش ساڵ بوو
هیچ بایەکی لە هیچ لایەکەوە پێدا تێپەڕ نەدەبوو.

ئەو شاعیرە بە کێوان کەوت،
بۆ یەکەمین جار (دووای چل و شەش ساڵ)
بای لەگەڵ خۆیدا
هینایە شار.

۱۹۸٥: ورمێ

For Hêmin

There was a poet
living in a city
where no wind had blown from any direction
for forty-six years.

That poet wound up in the mountains,
and for the first time (after forty-six years)
he brought the wind
back to the city.

1985: Urmia

بۆ قوبادی جەلی زادە

قوبادی جەلی زادە دوو جاران لە حەمامی ژنان دەرکراوە؛
یەکەم جار:
کاتێ تەمەنی گەیشتۆتە حەفت هەشت سالان و
ژنە حەمامچییەکە بە دایکی گوتووە:
"کوڕەکەتان گەورە بووە و
تەماشای مەمک و قەد و گیپالی ژنان دەکا
بەسیە، چیتر مەیهێنە حەمام!"
دووەم جاریش:
لە تەمەنی چل و پێنج سالیدا
ڕۆژێک بەڕاستی حەزی کردبوو
بچێ تەماشای
مەمک و
قەد و گیپالی ژنان بکا... بۆ ئەوەی
شیعرێکی دیکەی
جوانتر
بۆ ژن بنووسێ!

For Qubadi Jali Zadeh

Qubadi Jali Zadeh has been expelled from the women's baths twice.
The first time:
when he turned seven or eight and
the woman attendant told his mother,
"Your son has grown up and
stares at the women's breasts, figures, and bellies.
Enough! Don't bring him to the baths anymore!"
The second:
at the age of forty-five
when one day he really wanted
to stare at
the women's breasts,
figures, and bellies . . . in order to
write another,
more beautiful poem
for women!

بۆ ئێمێڵی برۆنتی

هەبوو نەبوو سێ سیۆ هەبوو.
یەکێکیان سوور
یەکێکیان زەرد
یەکێکیان سەوز.
هەرسێکیان، یەک لە یەکتر جوانتر.

یەکەمیان خورا.
دووەمیان دزرا.
ئەوەی تریشیان بە تەنیایی سەری نایەوە.

For Emily Brontë

Once upon a time, there were three apples.
One was red,
one yellow,
one green.
The three of them, each more beautiful than the last.

The first was eaten.
The second was stolen.
And the last laid its head to rest in loneliness.

بۆ لینین

هەبوو نەبوو
دوو پیاوی زۆر عاقڵ و دەوڵەمەند هەبوون.
یەکەمیان ناوی کارڵ مارکس
دووەمیان ناوی فرێدریک ئەنجڵز.

ئەم دوو پیاوە
سەرمایە و پارەوپوولێکی یەکجار زۆریان بۆ مابووە
یەکەمیان لە باوکییەوە، دووەمیان لە خێزانە پیرۆزەکەیەوە.

ئەم دوو پیاوە
پیر پیر دەیانویست پێش کۆچی دوایی کردنی خۆیان
ئەم هەموو سەرمایە و پارەوپوولەیان
بخەنە خزمەت ڕزگارکردنی مرۆڤایەتی
لەدەست برسێتی و نایەکسانی و نەهامەتییەکان.
چونکە دەیانزانی ئەگەر
ئەم هەموو سەرمایە و پارەوپوولە بخرێتە گەڕ
هەموو مرۆڤایەتی پێی دەحەسێتەوە.

ئەم دوو پیرەمێردە زۆر عاقڵ و دەوڵەمەندە
هەستان
هەر هەموو ئەم سەرمایە و پارەوپوولەیان
سپاردە دەست پیاوێکی گەنجی نەجیبزادەی
وەک خۆیان عاقڵ
دڵسۆز.
کە ناوی فلادیمیر لینین بوو.

لینین ئەم سەرمایەی ئەوانی سپاردە دەست شۆڕشی ئۆکتۆبەری ڕووسیا
شۆڕشی ئۆتۆبەری ڕووسیاش
بەوپەڕی ئەمانەتەوە سەرمایەکەی

For Lenin

Once upon a time
there were two wise and wealthy men.
The first was Karl Marx
and the second, Friedrich Engels.

These two men
inherited great wealth and fortune,
the first from his father, the second from his holy family.

In their old, old age
these two men wanted, before they died,
to use all their wealth and fortune
in the service of saving humanity
from starvation, inequality, and misfortune.
Because they knew if
all this wealth and fortune was put to work
all humanity could rest.

These two wise and wealthy old men
came
to trust a noble, young gentleman
as wise as them,
and loyal,
with all this wealth and fortune.
His name was Vladimir Lenin.

Lenin trusted Russia's October Revolution
with their money,
and Russia's October Revolution

سپارده دەست پیاوێکی کەتەی قەفەی سمێڵ زل.
ناوی ستالین.
باوکی قەساب بوو.

ستالین کەس نازانێ ئێستاش
چەندی لێ خوارد و
چەندی بەناوی یەکیەتی سۆڤیەتەوه لێ بەهەدەر دا.
بەڵام ئەویش لە کۆتاییدا
سەرمایەکەی سپارده دەست.
پیاوێکی دیکه به ناوی خۆرۆشۆف.

حەیف: پارەوپووڵ و سەرمایەکەی مامەپیرەکان
ورده ورده کەم دەبۆوه
ورده ورده لێی دەخورا، لێی دەدزرا، بەهەدەر دەچوو.

پارەوپووڵ و سەرمایەکه
هەر دەهات و دەستاودەست دەکرا:
خۆرۆشۆف سپاردیه دەست پیاوێکی دیکه به ناوی برژنێف.
برژنێف دایه دەست پیاوێکی دیکه به ناوی ئەندرۆپۆف.
ئەندرۆپۆف دایه دەست پیاوێکی دیکه به ناوی یەڵستن.
یەڵستن دایه دەست پیاوێکی دیکه،
ئەویش دایه دەست پیاوێکی دیکه...
تا گەیشته دەست پیاوێک
که ئەمرۆش هێشتا هەر لە ژیاندایه و
ناوی پوتین ه.

پوتین؛
کەس نازانێ ئەو سەرمایه و پارەوپووڵەی
ئەو دوو پیرەمێرده بەستەزمانه چی لێ دەکا!
کەس لێی ناپرسێتەوه ئەرێ ئەو سەرمایه و پارەوپووڵەی
ئەو دوو پیرەمێرده دڵسۆزەی مرۆڤایەتی؛ چییان بەسەرهات؟

entrusted it to a sturdy man with a bushy mustache.
His name was Stalin.
His father was a butcher.

And Stalin—even now no one knows
how much of it he bit off for himself,
nor how much of it he wasted in the name of the Soviet Union.
But he eventually
trusted another man with the fortune.
His name, Khrushchev.

Alas: the wealth and fortune of the old men,
little by little, decreased,
little by little, was nibbled away at, stolen, wasted.

The wealth and fortune
was passed over time from one man to the next:
Khrushchev entrusted it to another man, Brezhnev.
Brezhnev handed it to another man, Andropov.
Andropov handed it to another man, Yeltsin.
Yeltsin handed it to another man,
and he handed it to yet another man . . .
until it wound up in the hands of a man
who is still alive, and
his name is Putin.

Putin—
nobody knows what he does
with the wealth and fortune of those two poor old men!
No one asks, What happened to the wealth and fortune
of those two men, so loyal to humanity?

حەیف:
سەرمایەکەی مارکس و ئەنجلز
بەهەدەر ڕۆیشت...
مرۆڤایەتیش
لەناو هەمان برسێتی و نایەکسانی و نەهامەتییەکانی خۆی
تاکو ئەمڕۆش هەر
سواڵگەرێکە و
لەبن دیوارێک دانیشتووە:
دەستی پان کردۆتەوە و
غەریب غەریب
حۆڵ حۆڵ
تەماشای بورجی ئیڤڵ دەکات.

Alas:

the fortune of Marx and Engels

was wasted . . .

and humanity,

with the same hunger, inequality, and misfortune

still today,

remains a beggar

sitting at the foot of a wall:

hands outstretched and—

stranger stranger

fool fool—

staring at the Eiffel Tower.

بۆ د. عەزیز گەردی

"بەرەو کوێ دەڕۆی بەبێ بۆنی ژن و دەنگی ژن و تامی ژن... عەزیز
گەردی؟"

"ئەدی تۆ بەرەو کوێ دەڕۆی فەرهاد پیربال؟
بە خۆت و ژنەکەت و... پێنج منداڵ بەدوواتەوە؟"

"من دەچمە گۆڕستان، سەرێک لە قەبری باوکم دەدەین
لەوێشەوە دەچین فاتیحەیەک لەسەر گۆڕی داپیرم دەخوێنین.
دەی؛ بەرەو کوێ دەڕۆی، عەزیز گەردی؟"

"من بەرەو بەرزاییەکانی ویێزیرینگ ی ئەمیلی بڕۆنتی دەچم.
لەوێ لەناو باخچەکەی مارگرێت دووراس
ژووانێکی عاشقانەم لەگەڵ کلیۆپاترا هەیە.
لەوێشەوە لەسەر ڕێگەی خۆم
دەچم لە ماڵی فروغی فەروخزاد
پێکەوە شەرابێک لەگەڵ غادە السمان دەخۆمەوە.
شەویش دەچمەوە ماڵی جۆرج مەنسوور.
تا بەیانی لە باوەشی ژنەکەی ناپلیۆن بۆ خۆم، ڕاحەت
تێر تێر دەنووم."

For Dr. Aziz Gardi

"Where are you going without a woman's scent, a woman's voice, and a
    woman's taste . . . Aziz Gardi?"

"Where are *you* going Farhad Pirbal,
you, your wife . . . and your five children behind you?"

"I'm going to the cemetery, we're visiting my father's grave,
and from there we will go to recite the Surah Al-Fatiha at my grandmother's
    grave.
Now where are you going, Aziz Gardi?"

"I'm going to Emily Brönte's Wuthering Heights.
There in Marguerite Duras's garden
I have a date with Cleopatra.
From there, I'm on my way
to Forugh Farrokhzad's house
to drink a glass of wine with Ghada al-Samman.
And then I'll go back to George Mansour's house for the night.
I will sleep till morning, fully-fully comfortably
in the arms of Napoleon's wife."

بۆ نالی

شاعیر به هەموو ڕێگایەکدا، بێدەنگ
بێدەنگ
بێدەنگ دەڕوا؛
تەنیا لەسەر ڕێگەی شیعر:
سەما دەکا.

For Nali

Down every path the poet quietly
quietly
quietly walks.
Only down the path of poetry:
he dances.

بۆ حەمیدی قەووامی

بەبێ تۆ:
ناوم مەغدیدە.
تەمەنم پەنجا و چوار ساڵە.
سێزدە ساڵە ئاوارەی کەرکووکم.
مامۆستای ماتماتیکم لە گوندی قۆڕیتان ی نزیک هەولێر.
سێ ژنم هێناوە و پێنج مندالّم هەیە.
دوو هەفتە جارێک ڕیشم دەتراشم.
ڕقی دنیام لە عەترە.

لەگەڵ تۆ:
ناوم دەبێتە کامەران.
تەمەنم دەبێتەوە نۆزدە سالّ.
حەز دەکەم بچمە لای سەهۆڵەکە چاوڕێی تۆ بکەم تێ بپەڕیت.
لە ڕێکخراوی NDP کاردەکەم و مانگانە پازدە گەڵا وەردەگرم.
بەهاری داهاتوو بەتەمای گواستنەوەی تۆم و
بۆ مانگی هەنگوینی دەچینە ئەستەمبۆڵ.
هەموو ڕۆژێک کە دەچمە دەرەوە
ڕیشم پاک-پاک دەتراشم و
عەتری سکۆخیپیۆن نەبێ لە خۆمی نادەم.
لەگەڵ تۆ: خەونەکانم دەبنە ڕاستەقینەیەک.
لەگەڵ تۆ: پڕ دەبم لە شۆڕ و شەوق و شادی.
لەگەڵ تۆ: بە ناوەڕاستی زەوق و چێژ و بەختەوەری و گۆڕانییەکاندا تێپەڕ
دەبم.
لەگەڵ تۆ: عاشقترین عاشقم، کامەرانترین گەنجی دنیام.
لەگەڵ تۆ: ناویشم کامەرانە.

بەبێ تۆ:
ناوم مەغدیدە .
تەمەنم پەنجا و چوار ساڵە.
سێ ژنم هێناوە و پێنج مندالّم هەیە...

For Hamidi Qawami

Without you:
my name is Maghdid.
I am fifty-four years old.
I have been exiled from Kirkuk for thirteen years.
I am a math teacher in the village of Qoritan, near Hewlêr.
I've been married three times and have five kids.
I shave my beard once every two weeks.
I hate cologne with all my heart.

With you:
my name becomes Kamaran, "the happy."
I become nineteen again.
I like to go to Saholaka and wait for you to pass by.
I work at the NDP and make a salary of fifteen-hundred-dollars per month.
I plan to marry you next spring and
for our honeymoon we will go to Istanbul.
Before I go out every day
I shave my beard clean-clean and
if it's not Skorpion-brand cologne, I won't use it.
With you: my dreams come true.
With you: I will be filled with beauty, light, and happiness.
With you: I will traverse the essence of flavor, pleasure, joy, and song.
With you: I am the most loving lover, the most *kamaran* young man in the
    world.
With you even my name is Kamaran.

Without you:
my name is Maghdid.
I am fifty-four years old.
I've been married three times and have five children...

بۆ غەریب پشدەری

لەسەر زەویدا پرتەقاڵێک، لە دار پرتەقاڵێکەوە
چاوچاوانیی دەکرد لەگەڵ سێوێکی دارسێوێکی تەنیشت خۆی.

پرتەقاڵ و سێو بە حەواوە
عاشقی یەکتر، زۆر یەکتریان خۆش دەویست.

رۆژێک، هەفتەیەک
سێ هەفتە بەسەر شەیدابوونی هەردووکیاندا رابورد.

پرتەقاڵەکە لە دار پرتەقاڵەکەوە خۆی بەردایە خوارەوە
سێوەکەش لە دار سێوەکەوە خۆی بەردایە خوارەوە.

هەردووکیان بەسەر زەویدا گلۆر بوونەوە و
کەوتنە تەنیشت یەکتر.

پرتەقاڵ و سێوەکە بەرامبەر یەکتر
تەماشای یەکتریان دەکرد و رۆندک لە چاو.
بیریان دەکردەوە؛ مخابن:
لەسەر زەویدا تێگەیشتن
کە ژیان تراژیدیایە و عەشق ناکام؛
چونکە دیتیان
حەیف: کەسیان دەستیان نییە
تا ئەوی تر بگرێتە باوەش!

226

For Gharib Pshdari

On earth, an orange hanging from an orange tree
eyed an apple hanging from the apple tree next to it.

The orange and the apple up in the air,
smitten, adored each other.

A day, a week,
three weeks of growing passion sped by.

The orange threw itself from the orange tree
and the apple threw itself from the apple tree.

Both rolled across the ground and
stopped beside the other.

The orange and the apple faced each other,
stared into each other's eyes welled up with tears.
They were thinking, unfortunately:
on earth they understood
that life is tragedy and love is disappointment,
because they saw
alas: neither has hands
to embrace the other!

بۆ ڕۆدانی کوڕم
کاتێ تەمەنی دەبێتە ١٨ ساڵ

هاوڕێم
پاسەوانەکانت ناتپارێزن، بەڵکوو زیندانت دەکەن.

کوڕی خۆم، ڕۆدان گیان
کە گەورە دەبی
دەوراندەورت، هەمووی، دەبێتە پاسەوان
خۆیانت لێ دەکەنە فریشتە و
دێن پێت دەڵێن: ‑ ئێمە پاسەوانی تۆین، دەتپارێزین.
یەکێکیان دێ پێت دەڵێ:
‑ من مامۆستای تۆم، دەتپارێزم
‑ من ڕۆژنامەم، دەتپارێزم
‑ من مودیری ئاسایشم
‑ من دایکتم
‑ من باوکتم
‑ من وەزیری ناوخۆم... دەتپارێزم
‑ من کۆمەڵەم
‑ من سەرۆک عەشیرەتم
‑ من پۆلیسم
‑ من حیزبم
‑ من مودیرم
‑ من سەندیکام
‑ من مەلام
‑ من برای گەورەتم
‑ من ڕێکخراوم
...دەتپارێزم.

ئاگاداربە
ئەم پاسەوانە سەیر و سەمەرە و بەڕێزانە
ناتپارێزن؛ بەڵکوو دەیانەوێ زیندانت بکەن!

228

For My Son, Rodin
When He Turns 18

My friend
Your minders will not keep you safe, they will imprison you.

My son, dear Rodin
When you are older
Those who surround you, all of them, become minders
They will pretend to be angelic
They will come and tell you, *We are your minders, we will keep you safe.*
One will come to tell you:
—*I am your teacher, I will keep you safe*
—*I am a newspaper, I will keep you safe*
—*I am the director of the secret police*
—*I am your mother*
—*I am your father*
—*I am the Minister of the Interior . . . I will keep you safe*
—*I am the party*
—*I am the chief of the tribe*
—*I am the police*
—*I am the political party*
—*I am the manager*
—*I am the syndicate*
—*I am the mullah*
—*I am your big brother*
—*I am the organization*
    . . . I will keep you safe.

Be aware
These dear astonishing grotesques
Will not keep you safe—they want to imprison you!

لەو دەمەی دەتەوێ گوڵێک لە یەخەی خۆت بدەی

یان پرچت دابێنی

لەو دەمەی دەتەوێ بە یەکەمین کچی ژیانت بڵێی

– خۆشم دەوێی

لەو دەمەی دەتەوێ لەسەر تەختە ڕەشەکە بنووسی "سپی"

لەو دەمەی دەتەوێ لەسەر گەڵایەکی سەوز

بە قەڵەمی سوور بنووسی "زەرد"

لەو دەمەی دەتەوێ لەسەر گەڵایەکی زەرد

بە قەڵەمی سەوز بنووسی "سوور"

لەو دەمەی دەتەوێ لەسەر گەڵایەکی سوور

بە قەڵەمی زەرد بنووسی "سەوز"

لەو دەمەی دەتەوێ بیربکەیتەوە

لەو دەمەی دەتەوێ لە خۆت بپرسی:

"من هەم یا نیم؟!"

لەبیرت بێ:

پاسەوانەکانت خۆیان لێت مەڵاس داوە و چاودێریت دەکەن!

پاسەوانەکانت

بە خۆیان و کڵاشنکۆفەکانیانەوە

بە خۆیان و قسە خۆشەکانیانەوە

بە خۆیان و کۆبوونەوە ئیداری و ڕەسمیەکانیانەوە

بە خۆیان و ڕادیۆ و تەلەفزیۆن و عەینەک و تەسبیح و زانکۆ و مزگەوت و
قوتابخانە

و سەتەلایت و گۆڤار و دیوارە بڵندەکانیانەوە...

ناتپارێزن

ناتپارێزن بەڵکوو

خۆیان مەڵاس داوە و

لە کەمیندان بۆت

دەیانەوێ بتکەن بە کۆپیکراوی خۆیان

بتکەن بە کۆیلەی خۆیان.

When you want to fasten a flower to your lapel

Or to comb your hair

When you want to tell the first girl in your life

I love you

When you want to write *white* on the blackboard

When you want to write *yellow*

On a green leaf

With a red pencil

When you want to write *red*

On a yellow leaf

With a green pencil

When you want to write *green*

On a red leaf

With a yellow pencil

When you want to think

When you want to ask yourself,

To be or not to be?!

Remember:

Your minders are hiding from you, keeping an eye on you!

Your minders with their Kalashnikovs

With their nice words

With their management meetings and their bureaucracies

With their radio, television, glasses, prayer beads, universities, mosques,
schools,

Satellites, magazines, and high walls . . .

They will not keep you safe

They will not keep you safe but

They are hiding from you

And they are waiting in ambush

They want to make you a copy of themselves

Make you their slave.

ئاگاداربه

پاسەوانەکەت دێ پێت دەڵێ: ‒ مەڵێ نا!

ئامۆژگاریت دەکا دەڵێ: ‒ بڵێ بەڵێ!

هاوار دەکاتە سەرت:‒ جوان دانیشە!

چاوی لێت سوور دەکاتەوە:

‒ جارێکی دیکە تەماشای کچی خەڵک نەکەی، باش!

پاسەوانەکانت بەنەرمی و میهرەبانیەوە پێت دەڵێ:

‒ من دەتپارێزم

‒ ئەرکی پەروەردەیی منە بتپارێزم

‒ ئەرکی کۆمەڵایەتی و نیشتیمانی منە بتپارێزم.

پاسەوانەکانت فێری وەزن و قافیەت دەکەن

فێری **موطنی موطنی**... ت دەکەن

فێری پێنج جار نوێژی جەماعەت ت دەکەن

فێری ئەوەت دەکەن هەرگیز لە خەتی سوور نەپەڕیتەوە

پاسەوانەکانت فێرت دەکەن لەناو جەماعەت هەرگیز تڕ نەکەنی

بەڵام قرپ: قەیناکە

فێری ئەوەت دەکەن سوێر چییە، شیرین چییە، تفت چییە...

(دنیا چیتر زەمانیی منداڵیت نامێنێ کاتێ دەتگوت:

‒ بابە من ترشم پێ تاڵە

منیش دەمگوت: ‒ باش).

فێری ئەوەت دەکەن ئەگەر کچێکت خۆشویست

دەبێ یەکسەر بزانیت کە پێویستە

قەسر و قەمەرە و قەل و قبووڵی و قەڵای قیتی قیرتاو کراوت هەبێ

پاسەوانەکانت فێری حەیا و حورمەت و عەقڵت دەکەن،

فێری ئەخلاقت دەکەن.

پاسەوانەکانت

چوارچێوەیەکی بڵندی بەردیت بە دەورا دروست دەکەن و

ئیتر نابێ هەرگیز بیشکێنی!

Watch out
Your minder comes to tell you, *Don't say no!*
He advises you and tells you, *Say yes!*
He shouts at you, *Sit properly!*
They glare at you,
Don't look at anyone's daughters anymore, OK?
Your minder generously tells you:
—*I will keep you safe*
—*It is my educational responsibility to keep you safe*
—*It is my social and national responsibility to keep you safe.*

Your minders teach you rhythms and rhyme
They teach you "My homeland, my homeland..."
They teach you the mosque's five daily prayers
They teach you to not ever cross the red line
Your minders teach you not to ever fart in public
But burping: that is not a problem
They teach you what is salty, what is sweet, and what is bitter...
(Life is no longer like the days of your childhood when you would say,
Dad, sour tastes bitter to me
And I would say, *OK*)

They teach you, if you love a girl
You must know
You immediately need to have a palace, an automobile, turkey and rice, and a
    tall castle with a paved driveway
Your minders teach you shame, respect, and logic
They teach you morality.

Your minders
Mount you in a high frame made of stone
That you can never break!

پاسەوانەکانت زۆر نەرم و نیان، گەلێک موحتەرەم،
هەمووی پیاو ماقووڵ:
هەندێکیان عەینەکیان لە چاوە، هەندێک بێ عەینەک
هەندێکیان جبەیان لەبەرە، هەندێک سەترە و پانتۆڕ
هەندێکیان سەریان ڕووتاوەتەوە، هەندێک بوکڵەدار
هەندێک بێ سمێڵ، هەندێک سمێڵدار
هەندێکیان عەتر لە خۆیان دەدەن
هەندێکیشیان بۆنی تەگەیان لێ دێ.
هەندێکیان تەباشیریان لە دەستە، هەندێک دار حەیزەران
هەندێکیان بە قسەی خۆش
هەندێکیشیان زۆر توند و توورڕە.

پاشەوانەکانت لە هەموو شوێنێکن:
لەو شوێنەی حەزدەکەی پێ لەسەر پێتدابنێی و ناتوانی
لەو شوێنەی دەبێ پێ بکەنیت و حەزناکەی
لەو شوێنەی دەتەوێ بگریت و ناوێری
لەو شوێنەی حەزدەکەی ماچی دەزگیرانەکەت بکەی
لەو شوێنەی حەزدەکەی ڕەسمێک بگری
لەو شوێنەی حەزدەکەی پارچە مۆسیقایەک بژەنی
لەو شوێنەی حەزناکەی بنووسی
لەو شوێنەی حەزدەکەی بنووسی
لەو شوێنەی حەزدەکەی پڕ بە دڵ گۆرانیەک بڵێی
لەو شوێنەی حەزدەکەی تف بکەیتە چاوی مامۆستاکەتەوە
لەو شوێنەی حەزدەکەی خۆپیشاندانێک ساز بدەی
لەو شوێنەی حەزدەکەی بە وەزیری ناو تەلەفزیۆنەکەت بڵێی:
– ...ئاخر جەناب، ئاوها نابێ...
لەو شوێنەی گوێت لە رادیۆ راگرتووە و
مەسئوولێک درۆت بۆ دەکا
لەو شوێنەی حەزدەکەی هەڵسیەوە و ئەوێ جێ بیڵێ
لەو شوێنەی حەزدەکەی هەرگیز نەگەڕێیتەوە ئەوێ
لەو شوێنەی حەزدەکەی هەمیشە لەوێ بیت
لەو شوێنەی حەزدەکەی پڕ بەدڵ

Your minders are patient, intensely respectful,
All gentlemen:
Some wear glasses, some do not
Some wear the jilbaab, and some wear shalwar kameezes
Some are bald, some wear hairbands
Some do not grow mustaches, some do
Some wear cologne
Some smell like a billy goat
Some hold sticks of chalk, some hold bamboo canes
Some with nice words
And some fierce and angry.

Your minders are everywhere:
In a place where you wish to cross your legs but can't
Where you must laugh even though you don't want to
Where you wish to cry but don't dare
Where you wish to kiss your fiancée
Where you wish to take a picture
Where you wish to play music
Where you don't wish to write
Where you do wish to write
Where you wish to sing with all your heart
Where you wish to spit in your teacher's eyes
Where you wish to organize a protest
Where you wish to tell the minister on your TV,
  ... *Your Excellency, this is not how it goes* ...
Where you listen to a radio
To hear an administrator lying
Where you wish to stand up and leave
Where you wish to never return
Where you wish to stay forever
Where you wish with all your heart

قەشمەری بەو کەسە بکەی قسەت بۆ دەکا
لەو شوێنەی حەزدەکەی لە حزووری پاشایەک
یەک بە دەنگی خۆت جورئەت بکەیت و پێی بڵێی:
- جەنابی پاشا، تۆ ڕووتیت!

پاسەوانەکانت لە هەموو شوێنێکن:
لەناو پۆل، لەناو مزگەوت، لەسەر شۆستە
لە ماڵەوە، لەسەر جادە، لە دائیرە، لەناو باخچەکان...

پاسەوانەکانت تۆیان زۆر خۆش دەوێ و پێت دەڵێن:
- عاقڵ بە!
ئەگەر بە گوێت نەکردن، نەختێک توورە دەبن پێت دەڵێن:
- بە ئەخلاق بە!
ئەگەر هەر بە گوێیان نەکەی، هاوار دەکەنە سەرت
هەرەشەی فەسڵ کردن و نانبڕین و
لەوانەیە کوشتنیشت لێ بکەن!

پاسەوانەکانت کاتێ پێت دەڵێن "عاقڵ بە"، بزانە:
مەبەستیان ئەوەیە پێت بڵێن:
- یاخی مەبە؛ وەرەوە ڕیزی ئێمە!

کاتێ پێت دەڵێن "بە ئەخلاق بە"، مەبەستیان ئەوەیە پێت بڵێن:
- خۆت مەبە؛ وەکوو ئێمە بیربکەوە!

کاتێ هەرەشەی ترسناکیشت لێ دەکەن
مەبەستیان ئەوەیە کە
ئازادییە بەردارە هەلایساوەکەت لێ بستێننەوە!

پاسەوانەکانت بە هەنجەت و بەڵگەی جۆراوجۆرەوە دەتپارێزن
لە هەندێ شوێن بەناوی دینەوە
هەندێ جار بەناوی ئەمنی قەومیی کوردستانەوە
لە هەندێ شوێن بەناوی ئەخلاقەوە

To mock the one who speaks to you
Where you wish, in the presence of a king
To dare to say with your own voice,
—*Your excellency, you are naked!*

Your minders are everywhere:
In classrooms, in mosques, on sidewalks
At home, on the street, in offices, and in parks . . .

Your minders love you tremendously and tell you,
—*Be prudent!*
If you don't listen, they will get a bit angry and tell you,
—*Be ethical!*
If you still don't listen, they will shout at you
They will threaten to expel you, withhold your bread
Or even murder you!

When your minders tell you to *be prudent*, know that
They mean to tell you,
—*Don't be rebellious, cross back to our side!*

When they tell you to *be ethical*, they mean,
—*Don't be yourself, think like us!*

When they threaten you dreadfully
They mean to
Take away your full-grown freedom!

Your minders protect you with various excuses and evidence
On some occasions in religion's name
Sometimes in the name of Kurdistan's national security
On some occasions in the name of morality

هەندێ جاریش به ناوی عەشیرەتەوه
له هەندێ جیگه به ناوی ئیدارەوه
هەندێ جاریش به ناوی ڕێزگرتن و گەوره و بچووکییەوه
له هەندێ جیگه به ناوی پیرۆزییەوه
هەندێ جاریش به ناوی ئەمنی قەومی عێراقەوه
له هەندێ شوێن به ناوی پەروەردەوه
هەندێ جاریش به ناوی دابونەریتەوه.

پاسەوانەکانت خۆیان لێت مەڵاس داوه
دەیانەوێ هەمیشه به گوێی ئەوان بکەیت و
سنوورەکانی که خۆیان دایانناوه نەیانبەزێنی:
ماهێڵن دڵی خۆت خۆش بکەیت بێ ئەوەی گوێ بدەیته بەربەستەکان
ناهێڵن بژیت بێ ئەوەی گوێ بدەیته وەخته مردووەکان
ناهێڵن ڕەنگەکان و ئاوازەکان و نامەکان و بۆنەکان و گۆرانییەکان
سەرلەنوێ بەشێوەیەکی تازه دابهێنیتەوه
ناهێڵن خۆت بیت و ئازاد بژیت!

بەڵام تۆ هەمیشه له بیرت بێ:
کەمێک به گوێ نەکردن
دەبێته زۆرێک له دەسکەوت!

پاسەوانەکانت پارەت دەدەنێ
هەواڵەکانی جیهانت بۆ دەخوێننەوه
له ڕادیۆ و تەلەڤزیۆنەکانەوه گۆرانیت بۆ دەڵێن
پەنجەرەکانت بۆ دەکەنەوه
دەرگاکانت بۆ دادەخەن
معاشت دەدەنێ
دێنه هەر هەموو تازیەکانت
شووره و دیواری بڵند بۆ پاراستنی خۆت و هەموو هاوڕێکانیشت دروست
دەکەن
قەڵەمت دەدەنێ

And sometimes in the name of the tribe
On some occasions in the name of governing
Sometimes in the name of respecting your elders
On some occasions in the name of holiness
And sometimes in the name of Iraq's national security
On some occasions in the name of education
And sometimes in the name of tradition.

Your minders have hidden themselves from you
They want you to listen to them always and
Not to cross the borders they have built:
They don't allow you to be happy without considering the obstacles before
    you
They don't allow you live without recalling dead moments
They don't allow you to reimagine colors, melodies, letters, ceremonies, and
    songs
In new shapes
They don't allow you to live freely as yourself!

But always remember:
Just a bit of disobedience
Becomes countless achievements!

Your minders reward you with money
Read the world's news for you
Sing from the radio and TV for you
Open the window for you
Close the door for you
Pay your salary
Attend all your funerals
Build you towers and high walls to protect you and all of your friends
Give you pencils

تەباشیرت دەدەنە دەست
جانتات دەدەنێ
بەڵام ئازادی و دەسەڵاتت لێ دەستێننەوە!

وریابە هاوڕێم
پاسەوانەکانت هەمیشە دڕۆت لەگەڵ دەکەن
ناتپارێزن، بەڵکوو دەیانەوێ زیندانیت بکەن
دەیانەوێ بتکەنە کۆیلەی خۆیان، بتکەن بە کۆپیکراوی خۆیان.

پاسەوانەکانت
ڕێگاکانت لێ دەستێننەوە و کورسییەکت دەدەنێ
کتێبخانەکانت لێ دەستێننەوە و بەرماڵێکت دەدەنێ
ڕووناکیی زیرەوشانی کارەبات لێ دەستێننەوە و
چرایەکی حیزت دەدەنێ
دەست لەملانی و پیاسەی بەجووتەی ناو باخچەکانت لێ دەستێننەوە و
ئاڵایەکی کوردستانت دەدەنێ
عەشقەکانت لێ دەستێننەوە و
سیدییەکی نانسی عەجرەمت دەدەنێ
سۆز، نیگا، چرپە، ژووان، میهر و چاوچاوانیکانت لێ دەستێننەوە و
فیلمێکی خیلاعیت دەدەنێ
سەفەرەکانت لێ دەستێننەوە و
مەلعەبێکی پازدەهەزار کیلۆمەتر چوارگۆشەت دەدەنێ
پەساپۆرتەکەت لێ دەستێننەوە و
حەبێکی ئەنفلۆنزای طیورت دەدەنێ
قەتی، کۆتر، طیورالحب و چۆلەکەکانت لێ دەستێننەوە و
خەڵاتێکت دەدەنێ
خۆپیشاندانەکانت لێ دەستێننەوە و
ئیجازەیەکی سیاقەی تەزویرت دەدەنێ
مانگرتنەکانت لێ دەستێننەوە و
مانگێکی ڕەمەزانت دەدەنێ
ئاهەنگە گەرم و سەرمەستەکانت لێ دەستێننەوە و
"شەقامی سەهۆڵەکەت" دەدەنێ

240

Chalk
And bags
But they take your freedom and power!

Be careful my friend
Your minders always lie to you
They don't protect you, they want to imprison you
They want to enslave you, make you a copy of them.

Your minders
Take away the paths before you and give you a chair
Take away the libraries and give you a prayer rug
Take away the sparkling light of electricity
And give you a bastard lantern
Take away a lover's embrace and walks through the park
And give you Kurdistan's flag
Take away love
And give you an album by Nancy Ajram
Take away intimacy, glances, whispers, dates, affection, and eye contact
And give you a porno
Take away your journeys
And give you a 15,000-square-kilometer playground
Take away your passport and
Give you a pill for the bird flu
Take away the sandgrouse, doves, lovebirds, and sparrows
And give you some reward
Take away protests
And give you a fake driver's license
Take away hunger strikes and
Give you the month of Ramadan
Take away warm and drunken parties
And give you Saholaka Street

سەرتاپای سەری ساڵ و جومعە خۆشەکانت لێ دەستێننەوە و
مافی دەنگدانت بۆ هەڵبژاردنی ئەیاد عەلاوی دەدەنێ
ئاوی سازگاری ژیانت لێ دەستێننەوە و ئاوی حەیاتت دەدەنێ
سەرجەم کلیلەکانت لێ دەستێننەوە و حزبێکت دەدەنێ
سەرجەم هۆڵەکانی شانۆ و سینەما و مەلەوانگە و پێشانگەکان و
کافیتیرـیاکانی
ژووانەکانت لێ دەستێننەوە و
پارچە پلێتێکی قۆڕت دەدەنێ، لەسەر نووسراوە:
"تکایە
شت فڕێ مەدەرە سەر شەقام!"

ڕۆدان گیان،
من دڵنیام تۆ لەو کاتەدا، هاورێم
حەزدەکەی ئیتر
گوو لەو کۆمەڵگەیە بکەیت ئنجا دڵت خۆش دەبێ
من دڵنیام تۆ لەو کاتەدا
حەزدەکەی میز بەو کۆمەڵگایەدا بکەیت ئنجا دڵت خۆش دەبێ
چونکە لەو کاتەدا
تۆ گەورە بوویتە و دەزانی...
دەزانی کە پاسەوانەکانت ناتپارێزن؛
بەڵکو هەموویان
هەموویان دەیانەوێ زیندانت بکەن!

لەگەڵ هاورێی شاعیرم، هاشم سەراج، قسەمان لەبارەی پاسەوانەکان دەکرد و ئەم
شێعرە لەدایک بوو.

Take away every New Year's a Friday and
Grant you the right to elect Ayad Allawi
Take away the crisp water of living and give you the water of life
Take away every key and give you a political party
Take away the theater and cinema halls, swimming pools, exhibitions, and
    romantic cafes and
Give you a worthless plate, inscribed:
Please
Don't throw trash on the street!

Dear Rodin,
I am sure that by then, my friend
You will wish
To shit on society—then you will feel relieved
I am sure that by then you will wish
To piss on society—then you will feel relieved
Because by that time
You will be grown and you will know . . .
You will know that the minders don't protect you;
All of them
All of them want to imprison you!

*This poem was born from a conversation with my friend, Haşm Serac, about our
    minders.*

بۆ ئەلبێرت کامۆ

سەفەردەکا کەچی دەشزانیٰ
دەگەڕێتەوە هەمان شوێنی خۆی.

دەنووسیٰ کەچی دەشزانیٰ
نووسین تەنانەت یەک تاقە مندالّی برسیش تێر ناکا.

بە گەلْ خۆپیشاندانەکان دەکەویٰ
کەچی دەشزانیٰ ئەگەر ئەوانیش بێنە سەر حوکم
لەمانی ئێستا هیچ باشتر نابن.

بە ڕنووک،بە چنگەڕنیٰ، بەسەر شاخەکە دەکەویٰ
کەچی دەشزانیٰ کاتیٰ دەگاتە لووتکە
سەرلەنویٰ بەرەو خوارەوە گلۆر دەبێتەوە.

ئاو ئاو دەدات
کەچی دەشزانیٰ ئاو تا هەتایە هەر تینوویەتی.

دەژی
کەچی دەشزانیٰ –
دەشزانیٰ کە مردن هەیە.

For Albert Camus

He travels but he also knows
he returns to the same place as before.

He writes but he also knows
writing does not feed even a single hungry child.

He joins the protests
but he knows if they come to power
they will be no better than those who are in power now.

Scraping, grasping, he climbs the mountain
but he knows when he reaches the top
he will roll back down to the bottom.

He waters water
but he knows that water remains forever thirsty.

He lives
but knows—
knows death exists.

بۆ فەرهاد پیرباڵ

بەقەد ئیبلیسێک فێڵبازه
دوو بەقەد فریشتەیەک: دڵپاک

بەقەد شورطی مرووریّکی تازه تەعینبوو بیّ پارەیه
دوو بەقەد لویسی دەیەم: دەوڵەمەند

بەقەد تەلەفزیۆنێک زۆربڵێیه
دوو بەقەد کتێبێکی بێزار: بێدەنگ

بەقەد ئەسپێکی زۆر مەست هیلاکه
دوو بەقەد فیلێکی هیندی: هێز تێدا ماو

بەقەد مارکۆ پۆلۆ دنیادیدەیه
دوو بەقەد منارەی چۆلی: ساویلکه

بەقەد مانگی چوارده راستگۆیه
دوو بەقەد یاپراغێکی تەڕ: درۆزن

بەقەد پیرەپیاوێک دڵکوژاوەیه
دوو بەقەد گەنجێکی "لای سەهۆڵەکه": عاشق

بە قەد دکتۆر دەخیل ساغ و سەلامەته
دوو بەقەد مریشکێکی ڕانیه: دەردەدار

بەقەد شانەهەنگوینێکی باڵەکایەتی عاقڵه
دوو بەقەد سیاسەتی ئابووری ئەمرۆمان: بێ عەقڵ

بەقەد گومرگی سەر پەنیری تورکی زاڵمه
دوو بەقەد ماستی کوردی: مەغدوور

For Farhad Pirbal

He is as tricky as the Devil
and twice as purehearted as an angel

He is as moneyless as a newly employed traffic officer
and twice as rich as Louis X

He is as blathering as a TV
and twice as silent as a bored book

He is as tired as a drunken horse
and twice as energetic as an Indian elephant

He has as much worldly wisdom as Marco Polo
and twice the naïveté of the Choli Minaret

He is as honest as the full moon
and twice as slippery as wet yaprax

He is as dim hearted as an old man
and twice the lover a young man on Saholaka is

He is as healthy as Dr. Daxil
and twice as sick as a Ranya chicken

He is as wise as a Balakayati honeycomb
and twice as stupid as today's economic policies

He is as unjust as the duty paid on Turkish cheese
and twice as mistreated as Kurdish yogurt

بەقەد گۆرانییەکی ماهیر پاک و تەمیزە
دوو بەقەد شەقامێکی هەولێر: پیس و پۆخڵ

بەقەد سەرۆکێکی زانکۆ نەخوێندەوارە
دوو بەقەد قوتابییەکی کۆششکاری بەر چرا: زیرەک

بەقەد عەمیدێکی دکتاتۆر بێ حورمەتە
دوو بەقەد عیلمی مەنتیق: موئەددەب

بەقەد رۆژنامەیەکی ئەهلی ئازادە
دوو بەقەد سەتەلایتە کوردییەکان: دیل

بەقەد سەگێکی هار بە هات و هاوارە
دوو بەقەد گوجیلەیەکی بێ ساحێب: گوناح

بەقەد مارلین مۆنرۆ جەماوەری هەیە
دوو بەقەد گێزەرێک: تاک و تەنیا

بەقەد ئاڵای کوردستان ئازاد و دڵبڵندە
پازدە بەقەد کەرکووک: زەلیل و ژێردەست.

He is as clean as one of Mahir's songs
and twice as dirty and filthy as a street in Hewlêr

He is as uneducated as a university president
and twice as smart as a dedicated student beside their lantern

He is as disrespectful as a dictatorial dean
and twice as respectful as the science of logic

He is as free as an independent newspaper
and twice as captive as Kurdish cable channels

He yips and yaps as much as a rabid dog
and is twice as poor as an abandoned puppy

He has as big an audience as Marilyn Monroe
and is twice as lonely as a carrot

He is as free and high-hearted as the Kurdish flag
and fifteen times as wretched and oppressed as Kirkuk.

به بیرم دیَ...
۲۰۰۷

I Remember . . .
2007

به بیرم دئ سلێمانی که دارولمولکی بابان بوو
نه مهحکوومی عهجهم نه سوخرهکێشی ئالی عوسمان بوو

شێخ ڕهزا

I remember Slemani as home and domain to the Babans,
not judged by Persians, nor enduring Ottoman ridicule.

Sheikh Raza Talabani

به بیرم دێ ڕۆژانەم ڕووبعێک بوو.

به بیرم دێ، بۆ گەنم هارین، لەگەڵ دایکم دەچووینە دینگەکەی لای
تەکیەکەی شێخ عەبدولکەریم. چاوی ئەسپێکیان بەستبووە و ئەسپەکە
بە چاوبەستراوی بە دەوری دینگەکەدا دەسووڕایەوە و بەردە زڵەکەش
گەنمەکەی دەهاڕی. من بەزەییم بە ئەسپەکەدا دەهاتەوە.

بەبیرم دێ یەکەم فیلمی سینەمایی لە ژیانمدا بینیم فیلمی عەگدەل لوولوو ی
فەهد بەڵلان بوو، لە سینەما جوندیان... (که فیلمێکی قۆڕیش بوو)!

بەبیرم دێ عارەبی گامێشەوان، ماڵیان لەژێر پردی سەیداوە،
هەموو سبەینان قەیماغ و شیری گامیشیان دەفرۆشت.

بەبیرم دێ لە بن دیواری گۆڕستانی شێخەڵڵای هەولێر سەبەتێک گۆشتم
دادەنا و کیلۆی گۆشتم بە شەش درهەم دەفرۆشت.

بەبیرم دێ پاس مان دەگوت "ئامانە". وابزانم چونکە لەسەری نووسرابوو
"الامانه العالمه لمسلحه نقل الرکاب."

بەبیرم دێ تازه تەلەفزیۆن پەیدا ببوو، پرۆپیرەژن و منداڵە ورتکەی دراوسێ
دەهاتنە ماڵمان، بەدیار تەلەفزیۆنەوە دادەنیشتن تەماشای مسارعەی عەدنان
قەیسی و جۆن فرێزەرمان دەکرد.

بەبیرم دێ ئێوارەیەکی باراناویی قوڕ و چڵپاو
هەڵبژاردەی تۆپی پێی قوەی جەوی چوار گۆڵی لە هەولێر کرد....
لە کۆتایی یارییەکەدا هەمزە کەنناس م دیت: بۆ "هەولێری دۆڕاو" هۆن هۆن
دەگریا.

بەبیرم دێ لەمیعە تۆفیق، خاڵێکی تۆخ لەسەر ڕوومەت، لە تەلەفزیۆن
گۆرانیی دەگوت:
"شفتە و یبلعەجەل حەبێتتە وەڵڵا!"

254

I remember my allowance was a quarter.

I remember I would go to the column near Sheikh 'Ebidulkerîm's tekye with my mother to grind wheat. They blindfolded a horse and the horse circled the column and the big stone ground the wheat. I pitied the horse.

I remember the first movie I ever saw was Fahd Ballan's *The Pearl Necklace*, at Cundiyan Cinema . . . (which was also a bad film)!

I remember the Arabs who owned the buffalo, their house beneath the
    Seydawe overpass,
every morning they sold qaimagh, and buffalo's milk.

I remember I placed a basket of meat on the wall of Hewlêr's Shexalla Cemetery, and sold one kilo of meat for six dirhams.

I remember we called the buses "safeties." I believe it was because the slogan "safety first for the good of the passengers" was written, in Arabic, on the buses.

I remember when television had just arrived, old women and small children from the neighborhood came to our house and sat around the TV, watching Adnan Al-Kaissey and Géant Ferré wrestle.

I remember on a rainy evening of mud and sludge
the Al-Quwa Al-Jawiya Football Club scored four goals against Hewlêr . . .
At the end of the game I saw Hemze Kenas: he shed tear after tear for his defeated Hewlêr.

I remember Lamiya Tawfiq, a beauty mark on her cheek, singing on television, "I fell in love at first sight, I swear!"

بەبیرم دێ دە سەموونم بە دە عانە دەکڕی.

بەبیرم دێ باوکم دەیگوت:
"حەیدەرە فەندی، کە بەناو بازاڕدا تێدەپەڕی، هەمیشە گۆچانێکی دەسک
زێڕی بەدەستەوە دەگرت و عەبایەکی عارەبانی بەسەر شانی خۆیدا دەدا...
سامێکی زۆری هەبوو."

بەبیرم دێ لەگەڵ منداڵان هاوارمان دەکرد:
"مام جەلال پێمان تەزی
نامانەوێ لامەرکەزی."

بەبیرم دێ دەیانگوت: "عەدنان قەیسی جاسووسە."
بەبیرم دێ منداڵ بووین دەمانگوت:
"عارەب عێنی
گووی دەکوڵێنی
لۆ ڕدێنی."

بەبیرم دێ گۆرانیی "لاخەبەری" فازڵ عەواد، کاتێ بڵاوبۆوە شۆڕەتێکی
زۆری پەیدا کرد. ئێمە نەشماندەزانی چ دەڵێ، بەڵام ئەزبەرمان کردبوو:
"لا خەبەر
لا خەبەر لا،
چەفییە لا،
حامز حلوو؛ لا شەربەت."

بەبیرم دێ دەیانگوت: "لە بەغدا پیاوێک پەیدابووە بە تەور هەڵدەکوتێتە سەر
ماڵان و خەڵک هەلا هەلا دەکات." لە تەلەفزیۆنیش ڕووداوەکانیان پیشان دا.
پیاوەکە ناوی ئەبوو طەبەر بوو.

بەبیرم دێ تازە مۆدیلی خەنافس دەرچووبوو. ڕۆستەمی برادەرم لاعیب
بوو، خەنافسی بەردابۆوە. مام عەبدوڵڵای باوکی، ماست فرۆش بوو. کاتێ
دەچوومە دووی ڕۆستەم، باوکی دەیگوت: "کوڕم بۆتە جولەکە."

I remember I bought ten pieces of bread for ten pennies.

I remember my father saying,
"Ḧeyder Fendî, when he walked through the bazaar, always carried a golden-
gripped cane and an Arab abaya over his shoulders . . .
he was very frightening."

I remember we were chanting with the other children,
"Mam Jalal, numbed by the nation!
We don't want decentralization!"

I remember they were saying, "Adnan Al-Kaissey is a spy."
I remember we were children saying,
"Haven't you heard?
The Arab cooks a turd
to rub in his beard."

I remember the song "No News" by Fadil Awad. When it came out, it
became quite famous. We didn't even know what it said, but we had
memorized it:
"La khabar,
la khabar la,
chafiyya la,
ḥamiḍ ḥiluw, la sharbat."

I remember they said, "A man has shown up in Baghdad, breaking into
houses with an ax and chopping people into pieces." And they showed the
incidents on TV. The man's name was Abu Tubar.

I remember sideburns were a new trend. My friend Rostem was an athlete, and
he grew sideburns. His father, Mam 'Ebidulla, was a yogurt vendor. When I
would go to pick up Rostem, his father said, "My son has become a Jew."

بەبیرم دێ "سایلۆی هەولێر" ئەو کاتە لە بنی دنیایی بوو...
بەبیرم دێ، دایکم دەیگوت:
"یاخوا رەزا شا تەختت وەرگەرێ
کورم گەورە کرد بردت لۆ شەرێ."

بەبیرم دێ مستۆ قەطعەی دیعایەی فلیمی سینەمای لەسەر شانی خۆی
دادەنا و پرۆپاگەندەی بەناو بازاردا بۆ فلیمەکە بڵاودەکردەوە. کاغەزی
دیعایەی. دەدایە هەموو کەسێک،
تەنیا نەیدەدایە من، "چونکە مندال بووم."

بەبیرم دێ تۆما فەندی، مامۆستایەکی مەسیحی بوو، لە پۆلی یەکەمی
سەرەتایی مەکتەبی زانین، لە گەرەکی تەیراوە، دەرسی حسابی پێ دەگوتین.

بەبیرم دێ دایکم بە ئۆرزدی باگی دەگوت: "روشدی بەگ."

بەبیرم دێ لە کاتی گەمەکردندا، لەناکاو مندالێک بە چەپڵەلێدان و قەشمەری
کردنەوە دەیگوت:
"کور لە ناو کچان
باب قالۆنچان."

بەبیرم دێ لەناو هۆڵی سینەما هەر کە گڵۆپ دەکوژایەوە، لە چل بابییەوە
خۆمان ئاودیو دەکردە هەشتا باوی. هەر کاتی کارەباش بکوژایەتەوە،
یەکسەر دەمانکردە فیکەلێدان و هاوارمان دەکرد:
"قەمبوور، قەمبوور..."

بەبیرم دێ لە خۆپیشاندانی ساڵانی ١٩٧٠ دا هاوارمان دەکرد:
"کێتان دەوێ لە کوردان؟
- مەلا مستەفای بارزان."

بەبیرم دێ "ئاوی کەسک و سۆر" لە جێی پەیکەرەکەی ئەمرۆی موسا
عەنتەر بوو.

بەبیرم دێ پەیکەرێکی موسا عەنتەریان لە چوارپریانەکەی بەرامبەر هۆڵی
میدیا دانابوو.

I remember "Hewlêr's granary" was at the edge of the world at that time . . .
I remember my mother said,
"Oh Reza Shah, may God upturn your throne.
I raised a son, you took him to war."

I remember Msto carrying film posters on his shoulder and promoting the films in the bazaar. He gave the flyers to anyone,
except me, "because I was a child."

I remember Toma Fendî was a Christian teacher in the first grade of elementary school at Zanîn School, in Tairawa, teaching us math.

I remember my mother called Orosdi-Back "Ruşdî Beg."

I remember during recess, when suddenly a child would clap, mockingly saying,
"She gave him a hug
Now his dad is a bug!"

I remember at the cinema hall, the minute the lights turned off, we left the cheap seats. And the minute the electricity went out, we instantly began whistling and shouting, "Qembur, Qembur . . ."

I remember, at the protests of the 1970s, we shouted,
"Who do you want from Kurdistan?
—Mullah Mustafa Barzan."

I remember "the green and red water" was where Musa Anter's statue is today.

I remember they placed a statue of Musa Anter in the roundabout opposite Media Hall.

بەبیرم دێ باوکم دەیگوت: "ناو حەمامی قەڵاتێ ئەجندەی تێدایە."

بەبیرم دێ قوتابیی ناوەندی بووم، شیعرێکم لەسەر کوژرانی کەمال
جونبوڵات نووسیبوو، لە میهرەجانێکی شیعر خوێندنەوەی قوتابیانی
ناوەندیدا خوێندمەوە. شیعرەکەم لە میهرەجانەکەدا بە یەکەم دەرچوو؛ قەڵەم
پەندانێکیان بە خەڵات پێشکەش کردم. د. عەبدوڵڵا حەدداد سەرۆک لێژنەی
ئەو میهرەجانە بوو. بۆ وەرگرتنی خەڵاتەکە، منیان بانگ کردە بارەگای
یەکیەتی نووسەرانی کورد کە لە تەنیشت سینەما سەڵاحەدین بوو. ئەو
کاتە یەکەم جارم بوو چوومە مەحفەلی نووسەرانەوە: دەترسام هەندێکیان
"مندالباز" بن!

بەبیرم دێ شاکری کوڕی قادر بەرێیەی دراوسێمان لەبەردەم گازینۆی کورد
و عەرەب لە گەرەکی تەیراوە کوژرا.

بەبیرم دێ لەگەڵ محەمەد خۆشناوی سکرتێری کاک نێچیرڤان بارزانی،
لەسەر ڕێگەی مەسیف، شووتیمان دەفرۆشت.

بەبیرم دێ دایکم دەیگوت: "کاتێ جوولەکەی هەوڵێریان دەردەکرد.
هەموویان دەگریان و دەڵاڵانەوە، دوعایان لە حکوومەت دەکرد و بە پۆلیسە
عارەبەکانیان دەگوت: -هەی ئیسلامی حیز و دز یارەببی خێر لە داهاتووی
خۆتان نەبینن، کە ئێمەی بەستەزمان ئاوها دەردەکەن."
دایکم دەیگوت: "ئێمەش بۆیان دەگریاین و دەچووین ئاوێنە و کەوگیر و
کەلوپەلەکانی ناومالی ئەوانمان دەکڕییەوە. وەیش..."

بەبیرم دێ شووعیەکان لە گازینۆ عەبۆ کۆبوونەوەکانی خۆیان ئەنجام دەدا.

بەبیرم دێ باوکم دەیگوت: "وەختی خۆی دایکم بە مریشکێکی قوندە و
فەردە گەنمێک مارە کردووە." وابزانم بە سوعبەتی بوو.

بەبیرم دێ یەکەم نەورۆز لە ژیانمدا کردبێتم نەورۆزەکەی دارەتوو بوو.
بارانێکی زۆر باری (ئێوارە، لەناو قەرەباڵغیدا بزر بووم و نیوەشەو درەنگ
بردمیانەوە ماڵەوە).

I remember my father saying, "There are jinns in the castle's bathhouse."

I remember I was a high school student, I had written a poem about the assassination of Kamal Jumblatt, I read it at a high school poetry festival. My poem won the festival's first prize; they gave me a pencil as a gift. Dr. 'Ebidulla Ḧedad was the president of the festival's prize jury. To receive the gift, they invited me to the office of Kurdish Writers Union, which was next to Salahadin Cinema. That was my first time being surrounded by writers: I was afraid some of them might be "pedophiles"!

I remember Şakr, our neighbor Qadr Berriye's son, was killed in front of the Kurd and Arab Casino in Tairawa.

I remember we sold watermelon on Masif Road with Mohammed Xoşnaw, Nechirvan Barzani's secretary.

I remember my mother saying, "When they banished the Jews from Hewlêr, they were all crying and mourning, they were praying that God would do something terrible to the government, and they were telling the Arab policemen, 'You, thieving, asshole Muslims, I pray to God that no good ever comes to you, since you have expelled a helpless people like us this way.'" My mother said: "We were crying for them, we went to buy their mirrors, their ladles, and their furniture. Waish . . . "

I remember the communists holding their meetings at Abo Casino.

I remember my father saying, "At the time, I paid your mother's dowry with a short-tailed chicken and a sack of wheat." I think he was joking.

I remember the first Newroz I had was Newroz in Daratu. Rain poured down (in the evening, I got lost in the crowd and late at night they brought me back home).

بەبیرم دێ پەیکەری زەلامێک، زۆر بلّند، لە چوار رِیانەکەی بەردەم مەلعەبی
ئەمرۆ هەبوو، پێیان دەگوت "هەیکەلی زەعیمی." بە چوارِرِیانەکەشیان دەگوت
"فلکەی زەعیمی."

بەبیرم دێ هەموو پێش نیوەرِۆیەکی پێنج شەممە، بەتایبەتیش جومعان،
عەسکەر لە حەمامێ دەهاتنە دەرێ و دەچوون لە چایخانەکەی ئەولای
مالّان، بەرامبەر حەمام سیروان، بەدیار تەلەفزیۆنەوە تەماشای سەمیرە
تۆفیقمان دەکرد. هەللّایەک بوو نەبێتەوە.

بەبیرم دێ تەلەفزیۆنی کوردیی بەدا تازە کرابۆوە: سەبارەت بەوەی هێندە
گۆرانی و بەرنامەیان نەبوو، هەموو ئێوارەیەک، هەمیشە، تەنیا و تەنیا
گۆرانییەکانی محمەد قەدری و گولّبەهار و نەسرین شێروانیی دەخستەسەر.

بەبیرم دێ پیاوێکی کەشخەی کەلّەگەت و رِێکپۆش لەناو بازارِی خانەقا
هەبوو، هەمیشە گولینگ جوانەکانی کەشیدەکەی دەخستتە سەر گوێی
چەپی: ناوی مەلّالّۆک بوو. دەیانگوت گوێی چەپی براوە. منیش مندال بووم،
لێم ببوە مەرەق: هەموو جارێ کە لەگەلّ باوکم بە بەردەم دەکانەکەیدا
دەگەرِاینەوە مالّ، حەزم دەکرد هەولّ بدەم گوێی مەلّالّۆک ببینم. ئێستاش
هەر نەمبینی.

بەبیرم دێ دایکم دەیگوت: فەزۆ خانی ژنی حەیدەرە فەندی، زێرِی ژنە
موحتاجەکانی بە رِەهن وەردەگرت و لە جیاتی ئەمە پارەی دەدانێ، بێ
سوود وەرگرتن. هەروەها دەیگوت: فەزۆ خان تاقە ژنێکی دەولّەمەندی
هەولێر بوو کە سووی لە خەلّکی فەقیر وەرنەدەگرت.

بەبیرم دێ باوکم دەیگوت: "مەلیک فەیسەلّ لە ١٨ی کانوونی یەکەمی ١٩٢٤
دا هاتە هەولێر، لە قەسری باداوە لە دیوەخانی مالّی مەلا فەندی دابەزی،
نوێژی جومعەشی لە مزگەوتی قەلّاتێ کرد."

بەبیرم دێ پۆلیسێک لە گەرِەکی تەیراوە هەبوو، ناوی عەریف عیسا بوو،
ئێواران لەپێش دەرگای حەمام خۆشناو رِادەوەستا. دەیانگوت: "کورِ و کالّان
سواری خۆی دەکا."

I remember a statue of someone, very high up, at the crossroads in front of today's stadium, they called it "the leader's statue." And they called the crossroads "the leader's roundabout."

I remember before noon particularly Thursday, and especially Friday, soldiers came out of the bathhouse and went into the chaixana next to our house, opposite the Sîrwan Public Bathhouse, and we watched Samira Tawfik on the TV. It will never be so bustling again.

I remember the Kurdish TV station in Baghdad had just started broadcasting: since they didn't have many songs or TV programs, every evening, without fail, they only played songs by Mħemed Qedrî, Gullbehar, Nesirîn Şêrwanîy.

I remember there was a sharp, tall, broad-shouldered man at Khanqah Bazaar, and he always put the tassels of his turban over his left ear: his name was Melalok. They said his left ear had been cut off. And as I was a child, it became an obsession: every time we went back home, walking by his shop, I tried to get a glimpse of Melalok's ear. And I never saw it.

I remember my mother saying Fezo Xan, Ħeyder Fendî's wife, took needy women's gold as collateral and gave them money, without any interest. She also said: Fezo Xan was the only rich woman in Hewlêr who didn't accept interest from the poor.

I remember my father saying, "King Faysal came to Hewlêr on December 18th, 1924. He stayed at Badawa Castle, in Mullah Fendî's guest room, and he performed his Friday prayers at the citadel mosque."

I remember there was a policeman in Tairawa, his name was Corporal 'Îsa. In the evenings, he would stand in front of the door of Xoşnaw Bathhouse. They said: "he lets young, underage boys ride him."

بەبیرم دێ بە چایخانەی ئێستای مەچکۆیان دەگوت "چایخانەی میر هەڵئ."

بەبیرم دێ "پەست" لە هەولێر زۆر جوان بوون. وابزانم هاتوچۆی بەینی هەولێر و گوندەکانیان دەکرد.

بەبیرم دێ کۆتر بە سێ درهەم بوو.

بەبیرم دێ دایکم لە ماڵیوە هەمیشە دەسکە کەوگیرێکی پیشان دەدام و دەیگوت: "ئەم کەوگیرەم بە نیو رەپیە لەو جوولەکە کڕییەوە کە حکوومەت نەفیی کردن بەرەو ئیسرائیل."

بەبیرم دێ ئێوارەیەک لە سینەما سیروان، لە چل باوی دانیشتبووم. هەر کە گڵۆپەکان کوژانەوە و فلیم دەستی پێکرد، پیاوێک لە تەنیشتم، لەناو تاریکییەکەوە بێ خشپە دەستی بۆپ رانم دریژ کرد. ترسام. هەستام چوومە دەرەوە.

بەبیرم دێ سەردەمێک ئەگەر بتویستایە هێلکە بکڕی، دەبووایە دەستەیەک شقارتەشی لەگەڵ بکڕی.

بەبیرم دێ مەحموود زامدار گۆشەیەکی لە رۆژنامەی **هاوکاری** هەبوو، بە ناونیشانی "دەنگێ."

بەبیرم دێ عەونی یووسف جارێکیان گوتی: "یەکەم ئوتومبیل کە هاتە هەولێر، لە ساڵی ١٩١٥بوو، ئەڵمانیە هاوپەیمانەکانی عوسمانیەکان هێنابوویان."

بەبیرم دێ چایخانەیەک لەناو بازار هەبوو، پێیان دەگوت "چایخانەی مەلا مەولوودی." هەر کەسێک غەریب و خانەبەکۆڵ و بێماڵ بووایە، یان ئەوانەی لە ژنی خۆیان عاجز دەبوون و بێزاربوون، یان ئەوانەی شەوان ماڵیان دڵۆپەی بکردایە، دەهاتن تا دەمەوبەیانی لەوێ دەمانەوە.

بەبیرم دێ: هەر هەموو هەولێر گەراباى، یەک محەجەبەت نەدەدیتەوە!

I remember they called what is now Machko Chaixana "Mîr Hella Chaixana."

I remember the "pest" in Hewlêr were beautiful. I believe they transported people between Hewlêr and the villages.

I remember doves cost three dirhams.

I remember my mother always showing me the handle of her ladle, saying, "I bought this ladle for half a rupee from the Jews who were exiled to Israel."

I remember an evening at Sîrwan Cinema. I was sitting in the cheap seats. The minute the lights turned off and the film started, from the darkness, without even a rustle, a man beside me stretched his hands toward my thigh. I got scared. I stood up and left.

I remember a period of time when if you wanted to buy eggs, you needed to buy a box of matches with it.

I remember Meḣmûd Zamdar wrote a column called "A Voice" for the *Hawkarî* newspaper.

I remember 'Ewnî Yûsf once said, "The first automobile to reach Hewlêr arrived in 1915, brought by the German forces in coalition with the Ottomans."

I remember there was a chaixana in the bazaar, they called it the "Chaixana of Mullah Mewlûdî." Any stranger, traveler, or homeless man, or those who had fought with their wives and were tired, or those whose houses leaked could come and stay the night.

I remember: if you wandered around all Hewlêr, you wouldn't see a single woman with a headscarf!

بەبیرم دێ عارەبەکان، بە دیشداشەی سپییەوە، عەگاڵ بەسەر، بە خۆیان و
ژن و منداڵەکانیانەوە، لە گەڵی عەلی بەگ پیاسەیان دەکرد.

بەبیرم دێ لە مەلعەبی ئیدارەی محەللیی هەولێر تیپی هەڵبژاردەی تۆپی
پێی سلێمانی، دوو بە یەک، لە هەولێری بردەوە. بووە شەڕ و قیامەتێک
نەبێتەوە. دوو کەس کوژران و دەیان کەسیش بریندار بوون و ڕاگوازرانەوە
خەستەخانە.

بەبیرم دێ تەلەفزیۆن تازە دەرچووبوو:
"سیو... سیو... سیولا لاری.
لاری و لاری و سیولا لاری."

بەبیرم دێ، دوای بڵاوبوونەوەی گۆرانییەکەی "سیولالاری" بە چەند مانگێک،
کە ثلاث اضواء المسرح دەریانکردبوو، محەمەد ئەحمەد ئێربیلی گۆرانییەکی
بە تورکمانی دەرکرد: "وەڵڵاە تەلەقزیۆن ئیستارەم، حەپس ئاڵتوونم
ساتارەم."

بەبیرم دێ دایکم دەیگوت:
"یەکەم دەرمانخانە لە هەولێر بەناوی دەرمانخانەی شیمال لە ساڵی ١٩٣٤
کرایەوە (پیاوێکی فەڵە بە ناوی پۆلیس میرزا جۆرج کردبوویەوە). ئەوکاتەش
هەولێر تەنیا یەک خەستەخانەی و یەک دختۆری لێ بوو."

بەبیرم دێ جێگای ئۆرزدیباگی ئەمڕۆ (بەرامبەر مەحکەمە) حەساریکی
گەورەبوو.

بەبیرم دێ تازە "مزگەوتی سپی" دروست کرابوو، ئێمە، منداڵ بووین،
دەچووین لەو ئاقارە چۆڵەی ئەوێ، میزمان لە کونە دووپشکان دەکرد:
دووپشک دەهاتنە دەرەوە و دەمانگرتن لەناو شووشەمان دەنان. لەولاشەوە،
لە پەنادیواری مزگەوتە سپییەکەدا، فەقێ و مەقێی گەنج تەنەکەیان لەژێر پێی
خۆیان دانابوو: ماکەریان دەگا.

بەبیرم دێ عبد الستار طاهر شریف بە دەمانچەوە دەهاتە کۆڕە ئەدەبییەکان.

بەبیرم دێ شێرزاد عبدالرحمن یەکەم گۆرانیی خۆی لە تەلەفزیۆن تۆمار
کرد:

I remember the Arabs, with their white dishdashas, agal on their heads, with their wives and children, they would walk through Geli Ali Beg.

I remember at Hewlêr Local Administrative Stadium, Slemani FC won a game against Hewlêr, two to one. It turned into an apocalyptic fight. Two people were killed and dozens of people were injured, taken to hospitals.

I remember television had recently appeared:
"Su . . . su . . . sulalari.
Lari wu lari wu sulalari."

I remember, after the song "Sulalari," sung by Tholathy Adwa'a El Masrah, had been out for several months, Muhammed Ahmed Erbili sang a song in Turkmen: "By God I want a television, I'll sell my saved-up gold."

I remember my mother saying,
"The first pharmacy in Hewlêr was named Shimal Pharmacy, and it opened in 1934 (a Christian called Policeman Mirza George had opened it). At that time there was only one hospital and one doctor in Hewlêr."

I remember that the place where Orosdi-Back is today (across from the court) was a big field.

I remember "the white mosque" had been recently built. We were children. We went to the empty lot beside it to pee into the holes where the scorpions lived: the scorpions would come out and we would catch them, keeping them in jars. On the other side of the white mosque, next to the wall, young feqês and whatnot stood on top of oil tins: they were fucking mules.

I remember Abdulstar Tahir Sharif attended literary gatherings with his gun.

I remember Sherzad Abdulrahman recorded his first song on television:

"دۆستە دۆستە، دۆستە گیانی... دۆستە چاوەکەم." (شوهرەتێکی زۆریشی پەیداکرد.)

بەبیرم دێ چایخانەکەی گیوی موکریانی لە بن دیواری قەلاتێ بوو (بەرامبەر ئەسواق ئەربیلی ئەمڕۆ). حەزم دەکرد لای گیوی موکریانی ببمە شاگرد. ئەو ڕۆژەی لەگەڵ باوکم چوومە لای، قبوولمی نەکرد، بەڵام **لەیلا و مەجنوونێکی** بەدیاری پێشکەش کردم.

بەبیرم دێ باوکم لەگەڵ ڕەسوول گەردی پێکەوە، ماوەیەک، شورتەی حدوود بوون.

بەبیرم دێ شەمەندەفەر لە هەولێر هەبوو. جارێکیان بە چاوی خۆم لای منارەی چۆلی بینیم. بەبیرم دێ هەندێ جار لەگەڵ دایکم و ژنانی دیکە دەچوووینە لای قەسرەکان عەوتاولاغا، لەوێ جلوبەرگیان دەشوشت.

بەبیرم دێ بەدرێژایی حەفت هەشت سال، گەڕەکی تەیراوە و قەلات سەڕ و شۆڕێکی خوێناوی لە نێوانیاندا هەبوو. جارێکیان لە دەروازەی ئەحمەدیە، کە خەریک بووم دەچوومە مالی پوورم، بەدیل گیرام. لە سەرەوەی قەلاوە بە غلۆر کردنەوە توورڕیان هەڵدامە خوارێ.

بەبیرم دێ "عەونیه کۆر" و "نەجات خۆڕی" باشترین لاعیبی تۆپی پێی هەولێر بوون.

بەبیرم دێ ماوەیەک میسرییەکان بە لێشاو ڕژابوونە ناو مەیدانی عەمەلان. هەندێکیشیان دوکانی فەلافل و گەسیان دانابوو. (یەک دووانێکیان لە باری ئەربەئیللۆ بۆی بوون. برادەرم بوون.) تەنانەت میسرییەک کچە کوردێکی دەولەمەندیشی خواست. "ئەم فەزیحەیە" لە هەولێر دەنگی دایەوە.

بەبیرم دێ لە کۆتایی هەفتاکاندا، لەسەر دیواری مال و قوتابخانە و دائیرەکان، گەلیک جاران لەسەر دیواری ناوی ئاودەسخانەکانیش دەیاننوسی: "بژی کۆمەلەی ڕەنجدەرانی کوردستان."

"Doste doste, doste giyanî . . . doste çawekem." (And it became very famous.)

I remember Giwi Mukryani Chaixana was at the bottom of the citadel wall (opposite today's Aswaq Erbil). I wanted to become Mukryani's apprentice. The day I went to him with my father, he wouldn't accept me, but he gifted me an edition of *Layla and Majnun*.

I remember my father and Rasul Gardi together. For a period of time, they were soldiers stationed at the border.

I remember there were trains in Hewlêr. I saw one once with my own eyes near Choli Minaret. I remember sometimes, with my mother and some other women, we went to a place near to the Agha 'Awtawl Estate. They did their laundry there.

I remember for about seven or eight years there was a bloody fight between Tairawa and Naw Qelat neighborhoods. Once at the Ahmadi Gate, when I wanted to go to my aunt's house, I was taken as a captive. From the top of the citadel, they rolled me down to the bottom.

I remember 'Ewniye "the Blind" and Necat "the Layabout" were the best football players in Hewlêr.

I remember for a period of time Egyptians proliferated where the day laborers waited for work. And some of them had opened falafel and shawarma shops. (One or two of them found their place at the Arbaelo bar. They were my friends.) One of them even married a rich Kurdish girl. This "scandal" echoed across Hewlêr.

I remember at the end of seventies, on the walls of houses, schools, and offices, and often on the walls of public toilets, they had written: "Long Live Kurdistan Toilers League!"

بەبیرم دێ باوکم دەیگوت: "ئەحمەد چەلەبی بۆ یەکەم جار کارەبای بۆ هەولێر ڕاکێشا."

بەبیرم دێ خەلیفە سەعۆ سەرپەرشتیاری بەلەدیە بوو، ڕۆژ تا ئێوارە بەناو شەقامەکانی هەولێردا – بەسەر عارەبانەکانی ناو بازاردا دەسووڕایەوە بۆ ئەوەی لەناو جادە ڕانەوەستن: هاوار هاوار... بەردەوام هاواری دەکردە سەریان. ئەم پیاوە بەستەزمانە لەژیانی خۆیدا هێندە هاواری کرد تا لە کۆتاییدا قوڕگی تووشی سەرەتان هات و قوڕگیان بڕییەوە.

بەبیرم دێ دایکم دەیگوت: "حەزم لە کوڕ بوو. چوومە سەر گۆڕی سەید مەعرووفی باداوە، گوتم: – سەییدی حاڕ، سەیید مەعرووف، کوڕەکەم بدێ نیشانێکی بێ عەیبی هەبێ." دایکم دەیگوت: "تۆی دامێ بەو نیشانەی سەرتەوە کە ئێستا هەتە."

بەبیرم دێ دە سەموونی ئیعاشەمان بە پێنج عانە دەکڕی.

بەبیرم دێ ڕەمەزانان بۆ ڕۆژووشکاندن، گوێمان لە دەنگی تۆپ دەبوو: ئنجا ڕۆژوومان دەشکاند.

بەبیرم دێ مشکۆی گۆرانیبێژ، لەبەردەم سەیدەلیەی سەلاحەدین، پشتی دەدایە دیوار و لە بەرهەتاو ڕادەوەستا؛ دەستی ڕاستیشی لەسەر دەستی چەپی، کز کز، وەک ئەسیرێکی ئاسوودە تەماشای خەڵکی دەکرد.

بەبیرم دێ دایزە فاتمی پلکم دەیگوت: "کاتێ عەبدولکەریم قاسم هاتە سەر حوکم، ئێمەی ژنانی گەڕەکی گۆمەپیس و تەعجیل لەگەڵ ژنانی گەڕەکی جوولەکان و سەعدوونناوە... هەندێکمان بە پێچە و عەباوە هەندێکیشمان تەنیا بە عەباوە ڕژابووینە سەر جادەکان و هوتافمان دەکێشا:
– دەمانەوێ سەربەستی
پێچە و عەبا هەڵبستێ!"

بەبیرم دێ دەیانگوت: "ئازاد خەطاب و شێرۆ حەلیم و ئەبووزێد منداڵبازن." ئیدی، من شەوان لە ترسی ئەوان، هەرگیز بەبێ چەقۆ نەدەچوومە دەرەوە.

I remember my father saying, "Ahmed Çelebi delivered power to Hewlêr for the first time."

I remember Xelîfe Se'o was the administrator of the municipality. He scoured the streets of Hewlêr until evening, ensuring the carts at the bazaar didn't stop in the streets: shouting, shouting . . . always shouting at them. This poor man shouted so much over the course of his life that he eventually got throat cancer and so they cut out his throat.

I remember my mother saying, "I wanted to have a boy. I visited Seyd Me'rûfî Badawe's tomb, and said, 'Loving Seyd, Seyd Me'rûfî, give me a boy with a birthmark.'" My mother said, "He gave me you, with that birthmark on your head."

I remember we bought ten rations of samoon for a nickel.

I remember to break our fast during Ramadan, we listened for the sound of the artillery: and then we would break the fast.

I remember the singer Mishko, in front of Salahaddin Pharmacy, would rest his back against the wall to stand in the sun. With his right hand over his left, faint-faint, looked on the passersby like a happy prisoner.

I remember my aunt Daiza Fatim said, "When Abd al-Karim Qasim came to power, we the women from the neighborhoods of Gomepîs and Te'cîl, along with the women from the neighborhoods of Julakan and Se'dûnawe . . .
Some of us in our scarves and abayas and some of us in just our abayas went out on the streets, shouting:
'We want to be free
from the headscarf's tyranny!'"

I remember they said: "Azad Xetab, Şêro Ħelîm, and Ebûzêd are pedophiles." So, fearing them, I never went out without a knife at night.

بەبیرم دێ نەورۆزمان لە بەستۆرە دەکرد. دەمانگوت:
"بەستۆرە... ئاوی زۆرە."

بەبیرم دێ حاجی لەقلەقێک لەسەر لووتکەی مزگەوتی شێخەرەشکە هێللانەی
کردبوو.

بەبیرم دێ باوکم لەگەڵ قەسابە عارەقخۆرەکانی دیکەی برادەری، دەچوون
لە قەبرستانی شێخەللا عارەقیان دەخواردەوە (من هەنارم بۆیان هوورد
دەکرد).

بەبیرم دێ دایکم بە پەنجا دیناری دەگوت "دوو جار بیست و دە" دینار. بە
شەست دینایشی دەگوت "سێ جار بیست."

بەبیرم دێ یەکێک بیویستایە کەسێک ناشیرین بکات دەیگوت "دەڵێی گۆلکی
عوزێر پێغەمبەریت."

بەبیرم دێ نەمدەوێرا بچم لە گەرەکی کووران سەر لە ماڵی خاڵم بدەم،
چونکە "هەیاسە شیت" لەلای محەتتە ڕێگەمی لێ دەگرت.

بەبیرم دێ خوێری و سەرسەری بەیەکتریان دەگوت: "ئیسکیف..."

بەبیرم دێ دایکم دەستەکانی تووشی نەخۆشی وشکەبیرۆ هاتبوو. چەندین
دکتۆرمان پێکرد، هەر چاک نەبۆوە، چووینە لای ئەحمەد تەبیبی باوکی
فوئاد ئەحمەدی گۆرانیبێژ، دەرمانێکی لە ڕۆنی دارگەزی قرچاو بۆ گرتەوە.
یەکسەر چاک بووەوە.

بەبیرمن دێ دەرویش ماریان دەگرت و دووپشکیان دەخوارد. لە
ناوەراستی بازار زەرگیان لە خۆ دەدا؛ شیریان لە زگی خۆیان رادەکرد لە
پشتیان دەهاتە دەری...

بەبیرم دێ ئەگەر داوای پارەیەکی زۆرم لە باوکم بکردایە بۆ خەرج کردن،
دایکم لێم توورە دەبوو، دەیگووت: "خۆ کوری حەمە قەدۆی مووسلێ نیت..."

I remember we celebrated Newroz in Bastora, saying,
"Bastora . . . is rich in water."

I remember a stork nested at the top of Shekh Rashka Mosque.

I remember my father with his other arak-drinking, butcher friends. They
would go to Shexalla Cemetery and drink arak (I deseeded pomegranates
for them.).

I remember my mother called fifty dinars "two twenties and a ten" dinars.
And called sixty dinars "three twenties."

I remember if someone wanted to call someone ugly, they would say "you
look like the prophet Uzair's donkey."

I remember I couldn't go and visit my uncle in the Kuran neighborhood
because "Hayas the Madman" would stop me near the depot.

I remember do-nothings and vagabonds called each other: "Iskif . . . "

I remember my mother's hands were inflamed with eczema. We had her visit
many doctors, but they would not heal. We went to Ahmad Tabib, the father
of Fuad Ahmad, the singer, and he made a medicine out of sizzled turmeric
oil. They were healed instantly.

I remember dervishes were catching snakes and eating scorpions. In the
middle of bazaar they whipped themselves; they plunged swords into their
stomachs that would come out through their backs . . .

I remember if I asked for much spending money, my mother would get
angry, saying, "You are not the son of Hamu Al-Qadu of Mosul . . . "

بەبیرم دێ شتێک لە هەولێر هەبوو، ناوی بەخۆکە، تەسبییحێکی لەدەست:
ناوی شتتەکانی دەژمارد.

بەبیرم دێ لە گەڕەکی تەیراوە، لە مزگەوتی کوێتی، بانگم دەدا.

I remember a madman in Hewlêr. His name was Bexoke. With prayer beads in his hand, he counted the names of the mad.

I remember in the neighborhood of Tairawa, at the Kuwaiti Mosque, I sang the call to prayer.

کتێبی خەونەکان
٢٠٠٩

The Book of Dreams
2009

مەدام بۆڤاری

ئەگەر خەونت دیت پێڵاوی خۆشەویستەکەت
بە دیواری ژوورەکەی خۆتەوە هەڵواسیوە و تەماشای دەکەی
ئەوا لە داهاتوودا جوانیی خۆشەویستەکەت دەبێتە وانەیەک
لە کۆلێژی هونەرە جوانەکاندا دەگوترێتەوە.

ئەگەر خەونت دیت دەزگیرانەکەت لەناکاو
مێردی بە کوڕە دەوڵەمەندێک کرد
مانای وایە
ئەو دەبێتە تابلۆیەکی ناودار
تۆش بە بێکەسی، سەر دەنێیتەوە.

پیاو هێزێکن
ژن بۆ خۆیانی دەبەن.

Madame Bovary

If you dream of your lover's shoes hanging
on the wall of your room and you admire them
then in the future your beloved's beauty will be a lesson
taught at the College of Fine Arts.

If you dream your fiancée suddenly
marries a rich boy
it means
she's going to become a famous painting
and you will die alone.

Men are strength
women take for themselves.

کۆدی داقنشی

ئەگەر خەونت دیت سێوێکی سوور زەرد هەڵگەڕابوو
مانای وایە تۆ بەختت ڕەشە.

ئەگەر خەونت دیت سێوێکی ڕەش
لەسەر مێزێکی مزر داندرابوو
مانای وایە تۆ
دەبێ لەمەودووا خۆت فێربکەی:
چۆن لەززەت لە تەماشاکردنی ژن وەربگریت.

ئەگەر خەونت دیت سێوێکی شین
لەسەر مێزێکی مۆر داندرابوو؛
مانای وایە تۆ
دەبێ ئیتر خۆت فێربکەی:
چۆن چێژ لە تامکردنی ژن وەربگریت.

ئەگەر خەونت دیت ژنێکی نارنجی
عەینەن سێوێکی سەوز
کراسە پەمەییەکەی خۆی داکەند و
لەبەردەمتا خۆی ڕووت کردەوە؛
مانای وایە تۆ
کاتی هاتووە... دەبێ عاشق بیت!

ژن خەونێکی جوانن
"پیاو" دەیانبینن.

280

The Da Vinci Code

If you dream of a red apple turned yellow
it means you have bad luck.

If you dream of a black apple
placed on a sour table
it means from now on
you must then teach yourself:
how to savor observing women.

If you dream of a blue apple
placed on a purple table
it means you
must then teach yourself
how to enjoy tasting women.

If you dream of an orange woman
like a green apple
taking off her pink dress
undressing before you
it means
it's time . . . you must fall in love!

Women are beautiful dreams
"men" dream.

جەدوەل زەرب

کەروێشک خەون بە گێزەرەوە دەبینێ
قاز بە گەنمەشامییەوە
پشیلە بە ماست
مشک بە نانەوردە
بەراز بە بەروو
ورچ بە ماسی
مەیموون بە مۆز
سەگ بە ئێسقان
منیش بە تۆ.

Multiplication Table

Rabbits dream of carrots
Geese of corn
Cats of yogurt
Mice of breadcrumbs
Pigs of acorns
Bears of fish
Monkeys of bananas
Dogs of bones
And I of you.

ماتریکس

خەون بە گەڵاوە ببینی، خراپە.
خەون بە ئاونگ و تکەی هەورەوە ببینی، ساویلکانەیە.
خەون بە گوڵەوە ببینی، خراپتر.
خەون بە پۆڕ و قورینگانەوە ببینی، زۆر خراپتر.
خەون بە پەپوولەوە ببینی خراپ نیە، بەڵام.
هیچ سوودێکی ئەوتۆی نییە.
خەون بە مانگەوە ببینی هەر زۆر زۆر خراپە.
خەون بە ئەستێرەکانەوە ببینی، لە هەموویان خراپتر.

خەون بە خۆتەوە ببینە:
لە ناوەڕاستی شەقامێک
ئوتومبیل و باڵەخانە و ئەنتەرنێت و بۆیاخچی و پۆلیس و خەستەخانە و
ڕافیعە و ڕێبوارەکان؛ تەنانەت مودیر زەڕپیە و شورتی مرووڕەکانیش...
ستایشت بکەن!

The Matrix

If you dream of leaves, it's bad.
If you dream of dew and drops of cloud, it's naïve.
If you dream of flowers, it's worse.
If you dream of black partridges and cranes, much worse.
If you dream of butterflies, it's not bad, though.
It's not good for much.
If you dream of the moon, it's so very, very bad.
If you dream of the stars, worst of all.

Dream of yourself:
in the middle of the street
cars, buildings, the internet, painters, police officers, hospitals,
cranes, and travelers—even tax collectors and traffic cops . . .
praise you!

ئێوارەخوانێکی سەر سەوزەگیا

بەنەرمییەوە
یەک دڵۆپ ئاو بتکێتە سەر ڕوومەتی دڵدارەکەت:
بۆئەوەی شەو دڵدارەکەت خەون ببینێ کە لە ئیتاڵیا
لەگەڵ تۆ
لە شاری ڤینیز
لە گازینۆیەکی قەراغ دەریا
پێکەوە شەرابی مارتینی دەخۆنەوە
شەلاڵی زەوق لە باوەش یەکتر.

دەی...
شووشەیەک عەتر لە لووتی خۆشەویستەکەت نزیک بخەرەوە
بۆئەوەی شەو خەون ببینێ
کە لەگەڵ تۆ
لە ئەستەمبۆڵ
لەناو مەغازەیەکی بۆن و بەرامدا
مستەر بین شووشەیەک گۆلاوتان پێ دەفرۆشێت و
پێدەکەنن.

دەی... جورئەت بکە
پەنجە بە تاڵێکی قژی دڵدارەکەتدا بهێنە
بۆئەوەی شەو
خەون ببینێت
کە لەگەڵ تۆ
لە ئەمستردام
چوونەتە شهر العسل:
لەناو باخچەی هوتێلێکدا
نووری مالیکی و بشار الاسد و عبدالله گول
هەرسێکیان بوونەتە خزمەتکارتان و
گلازێک دۆندرمەتان لەپێش دادەنێن.

A Dinner on the Green Grass

Gently
drip a drop of water on your beloved's cheek:
so that your lover dreams of being in Italy
with you
at a seaside casino
in the city of Venice
drinking Martini & Rossi together
drenched in desire in each other's arms.

Come on...
Hold a bottle of perfume beneath your lover's nose
so that she dreams
that she is with you
in Istanbul
in a restaurant bursting with scent and flavor
Mr. Bean will sell you a bottle of rosewater and
you'll laugh.

Come on... dare
to stroke a strand of your sweetheart's hair
so that
she dreams
of being with you
in Amsterdam
You are on your honeymoon:
in a hotel garden
Nouri al-Maliki, Bashar al-Assad, and Abdullah Gül
have all three become your waiters and
place a dish of dondurma before you.

تەورات، بەندی چواردەهەم، دێڕی شەشەم

خەونم دیت پیر بوویمە
مندالٚ بوومەوە.

خەونم دیت کەلەپچە کراوم
مەچەکی خۆمم لاواندەوە.

خەونم دیت لێم دەدەن
هاوارم کرد.

خەونم دیت قورگم نەماوە
کەوتمە سەر نیگارکێشان.

خەونم دیت ڕەش هەلٚگەڕاوم
خۆم سپی هەلٚگەڕاند.

خەونم دیت توانای نیگارکێشانم نیە
دەستم کردە هاتوهاوار و گۆرانی.

خەونم دیت بەرگری لە هەق دەکەم
فەسلٚ کرام.

خەونم دیت خەریکە دەڕشێمەوە
چووم گووم کرد.

خەونم دیت فەسلٚ کراوم
کارێکی دیکەم دۆزییەوە.

خەونم دیت بەزۆر دەمنێرنە جەنگەکان
سەری خۆم هەلٚگرت.

Torah, Chapter Fourteen, Verse Six

I dreamed I was old
I became a child again.

I dreamed I was handcuffed
I soothed my wrists.

I dreamed they were beating me
I shouted.

I dreamed I had no throat
I began to paint.

I dreamed I turned black
I turned myself white.

I dreamed I couldn't paint
I began to shout and sing.

I dreamed I was defending the truth
I was fired.

I dreamed I was about to vomit
I went to poop.

I dreamed I was fired
I found another job.

I dreamed I was being forced to go to war
I fled.

خەونم دیت پارەم نەماوە
سەرسەری بووم.

خەونم دیت پارەی سەفەرکردنم نیە
بە پێ کەوتمە ڕێ.

خەونم دیت سەرسەری بوویمە
کەوتمە کارکردن.

خەونم دیت دەکەومە خوارەوە
فڕیم.

خەونم دیت گوریسیان لە مل ئاڵاندووم
گەرووی خۆمم لاواندەوە.

خەونم دیت خەریکە دەمرم
کەوتمە سەر نووسینی شیعر.

I dreamed I ran out of money
I became a bum.

I dreamed I didn't have the money to travel
I set off by foot.

I dreamed I was a bum
I began to work.

I dreamed I was falling
I flew away.

I dreamed that they had tied a noose around my neck
I soothed my throat.

I dreamed I was about to die
I started writing poetry.

بۆ ئەوەی ناوت بکەوێتە ناو قاموس الاعلام ەوە

ئەگەر خەونت بە بارانەوە دیت
تەنیا بۆ یەک درەخت بیگێڕەوە.

ئەگەر خەونت بە دەریاوە دیت
تەنیا بۆ یەک شاعیر بیگێڕەوە.

ئەگەر خەونت بە نانەوە دیت
تەنیا بۆ یەک برسی بیگێڕەوە.

ئەگەر خەونت دیت عاشق بووی
بۆ هەموو برادەرەکانت بیگێڕەوە.

To Get Your Name in the Encyclopedia

If you dream of rain
tell just one tree.

If you dream of the sea
tell just one poet.

If you dream of bread
tell just one hungry person.

If you dream you are in love
tell all your friends.

۲۷ پەرچەی ئێسک
۲۰۰۹

27 Pieces of Bone
2009

پێشمەرگەی پۆست مۆدێرن

پێشمەرگە قارەمانەکانی دوێنێ:
مەسئوولە گەندەڵەکانی ئەمڕۆ
شێرە هەمیشە بێدارەکانی دوێنێ:
پەرلەمانتارە نوستووەکانی ئەمڕۆ
پڵنگە هەڵمەتبەرەکانی دوێنێ:
پشیلە دابەستییەکانی ئەمڕۆ؛
بە گەنج و قوتابییانی ئەمڕۆ دەڵێن:
"مادام ئێوە پێشمەرگایەتیتان نەکردووە؛
بۆتان نیە ڕەخنە بگرن."

- ئەدی مەگەر هەموو بەیانیەکی ناشتا
سەعات و نیوێک بە پێ بڕۆیت تا
لە گوندێکی تر فێری "دارا..." بیت کە "دوو داری دی؛"
پێشمەرگایەتی نیە؟!

- مووچە عارەقاوییەکەت تەنیا
سەد و پەنجا هەزار دینار
چوار سنۆبەری وشکهەڵگەڕاویش بەخێوبکەی...
پێشمەرگایەتی نیە؟!

- لە تڕی سەگ چوونی قاچێکت لە بەرەبەیانێکی براکوژیدا
هەموو شەو بێ کارەبا
بێ پەساپۆڕت
بێ ئاو
بێ هیوا
بێ گندۆڕە
تەنیا چرایەکی لاچاو بریندار
دڵی ماڵەکەت بداتەوە!

The Postmodern Peshmerga

Yesterday's heroic peshmergas:

        today's corrupt officials

Yesterday's ever-vigilant lions:

        today's sleeping parliamentarians

Yesterday's attacking tigers:

        today's domesticated cats;

They tell today's youth:

"Since you have not served as peshmerga,

you are not allowed to criticize us."

—Well, if you walk for an

hour and a half every morning on an empty stomach

to study "Dara" in another village where he "digs a deep ditch,"

isn't that being a peshmerga?!

—Your sweaty salary is only

one hundred and fifty thousand dinars

and you tend to four dried out pine trees . . .

isn't that being a peshmerga?!

—Your leg has gone the way of a dog's fart one fratricidal morning

no power all night

no passport

no water

no hope

no melon

only a lantern with a wounded eye

comforts your house!

– به لایه‌یەکی موفلیسەوه ئاودانی باخچەیەکی تاریک
وەرنەگرتنی مووچه تەپوتۆزاوییەکەت بۆ ماوەی شەش مانگی برسی؛
خوشک و ژن و دۆتمامەکانت
ساڵی دوو جار سکیان پڕ بێ و
خەستەخانەیەکی ویلادەشیان نەبێ؛
بەبێ شوققه
بەبێ عەرزه
بەبێ گەرەنتیی تەندروستی
بەبێ سلفه
بەبێ بەرید
بەبێ تەنانەت کتێبخانەیەکیش
هەزاران ماسیی تینووش دەمیان بۆ پەیڤەکان کردبێتەوه؛
ئەدی ئەمه پێشمەرگایەتی نیه؟!

– پێشمەرگه خۆی
کرێی خانووی: پێنج سەد هەزار و نۆ سەد و شەست و شەش دینار
مووچەکەی تەنیا سەد هەزار و نۆ سەد و نەوەد و شەش دینار
بەدەم پاراستنی بۆڕییه نەوتەکانی کەرکووکەوه
له بەیانییەوه تا سی و یەکی مانگ
له سی و یەکی مانگەوه تا هێرش بردنێکی تازەی تورکیا
خۆزگه دەخوازیٰ تورکیا هێزرشیکی دیکه بکاتەوه سەر کوردستان
تا مووچه کۆنەکانیشی لەگەڵ وەربگرێت
له شەر دژی ئیرهابییەکانی فەللووجەش بەڵکو دوور بکەوێتەوه.
ئەدی ئەمه پێشمەرگایەتی نیه؟!

مێژوو، مێژوو، مێژوو...!
مێژووی بەسەرچووی تێهەڵدراو...!

مێژووی پڕ سەروەری بۆ خۆتان؛
میللەت ڕووناکی و نانی دەوێ.

—Watering a dark garden by a feeble light
not receiving your dusty paycheck for six hungry months;
your sisters, wife, and cousins
getting pregnant twice a year and
they don't even have a maternity hospital;
no apartment
no plot of land
no health insurance
no loan
no post office
not even a library
even if thousands of thirsty fish have opened their mouths to words,
isn't that being a peshmerga?!

—Peshmerga themselves
their rent: five hundred thousand, nine hundred and sixty-six dinars
their salary is only one hundred thousand, nine hundred and ninety-six
    dinars
to protect the oil pipelines in Kirkuk
from early morning until the thirty-first day of the month
from the thirty-first day of the month until Turkey's next attack
he wishes Turkey would attack Kurdistan again
so he could make his old salary
and so he could avoid the fight against the terrorists in Fallujah.
Isn't that being a peshmerga?!

History. History. History . . . !
History obsolete and banished . . . !

Keep sovereign history for yourselves,
the nation wants electricity and bread.

قەسر و قەمەرە و قاز و قەل و قبوولی و قەلا قیرتاوکراوەکان بۆ خۆتان؛
ئینسان ئازادی و ژیانی دەوێ.

ئەی شێرە هەمیشه بێدارەکانی دوێنێ؛
پەرلەمانتارە هەمیشه نوستووەکانی ئەمرۆ!
ئەی پلنگه هەڵمەتبەرەکانی دوێنێ؛ پشیله دابەستییەکانی ئەمرۆ
ئەی پێشمەرگه قارەمانەکانی دوێنێ؛ مەسئووله گەندەڵەکانی ئەمرۆ!
ئەسڵەن
ئەو پێشمەرگایەتییەی ئێوەی ناو شاخان
که شەش مانگ جارێک
تەنیا عەسکەرێک یان ئائیب عەریفێکتان دەکوشت
لەچاو ئەم پێشمەرگایەتییه برسی و هیلاک و پۆست مۆدێرنەی
ئەمرۆی ئێمه...
گەمەی منداڵان بوو.

Take the palaces and the cars and the geese and the turkeys and the rice and
    the castles with paved driveways for yourselves,
the people want freedom and life.

Oh ever-vigilant lions of yesterday,
today's ever-sleeping parliamentarians!
Oh attacking tigers of yesterday, today's domesticated cats
Oh heroic peshmergas of yesterday, today's corrupt officials!
Actually
your time as peshmergas in the mountains
when you only had to kill a soldier or a deputy sheriff
once in every six months
in comparison to this hungry, tired, postmodern peshmerga
of ours today . . .
it was child's play.

وەکو هێڵ ئازاد

‫- ئازادیت دەوێ؟‬
‫- هەرچی چوارچێوەیەکی لە دەوروبەرتە بیشکێنە و... وەرە دەرەوە!‬

‫- کارەبات نیە؟‬
‫- پەیڤە پەمەییەکان لەناو خۆتدا داگیرسێنە!‬

‫- کارت نیە؟‬
‫- لەسەر سنووری خەون و وەدیهێناندا قاچاخچێتی بکە!‬

‫- دەزگیرانت نیە؟‬
‫- جار جار بڕۆ باوەش بە درەختێکدا بکە!‬

‫- نیشتیمانت نیە؟‬
‫- سەری خۆت هەڵگرە: دڵنیام نیشتیمانێک دەدۆزیتەوە.‬

‫- پارەت نییە؟‬
‫- بەفر بخۆ، ڕێواس بخۆ، هێلکەی کیسەڵ، گەڵای دار بخۆ!‬

‫- پارەت نیە تەنانەت ئەنگوستیلەیەکیش بکریت بۆ یارەکەت؟‬
‫- لاسکە گیایەک هەڵگرەوە و لە پەنجەی یارەکەتی بئاڵێنە!‬

‫- پەساپۆرتت نیە؟‬
‫- ببە بە با، ببە بە ئاو، ببە ماسی؛ ببە پێ تا دەگەیتە شوێنی مەبەست.‬

‫ئافەرین بۆ ئەو عاشقانە،‬
‫ئافەرین بۆ ئەو سەرگەڤازانەی‬
‫بێ ئازادی و بێ دەزگیران و بێ کارەبا و بەبێ پارە و بێ پەساپۆرتیش‬
‫گەیشتنە قەراغە درەوشاوەکانی‬
‫ئیجە و سین و ڕاین و دەردەنیل!‬

As Free as a Line

—You want freedom?
—Break every frame around you and . . . come out!

—You don't have electricity?
—Light up the pink words inside you!

—You don't have a job?
—Become a smuggler on the border of dreams and creativity!

—You don't have a beloved?
—Go hug a tree every now and then!

—You don't have a homeland?
—Head out: I'm sure you'll find one.

—You don't have money?
—Eat snow, eat rhubarb, eat turtle eggs, eat tree leaves!

—You don't even have the money to buy your girlfriend a ring?
—Pick the stem of an herb and wrap it around your girlfriend's finger!

—You don't have a passport?
—Become the wind, water, fish; become a foot until you reach your
   destination.

Well done to the lovers,
well done to the adventurers
with no freedom, no betrothed, no electricity, no money, and no passport
they reached the shining shores
of the Aegean, Seine, Rhine, and Dardanelles!

گردە مژە

فی البدا کانت الکلمە

لە سەرەتادا گردێک هەبوو
گردێکی رەق و تەق
بێ هیچ درەختێک
بێ هیچ سێبەرێک
بۆیەش ژیانی هیچ تێدا نەبوو.

ئنجا وشەیەک پەیدابوو
لە خوار گردەکەوە
پاشان وشەیەکی تر
پێکەوە
چاویان برییبووە ئەو گردە رووتە
لە کۆتاییدا حەزیان کرد –
جەسارەتیان کرد بچنە سەر ئەو گردە
خۆیان بروێنن.

دوو وشەکە چوونە سەر گردەکە
رووت و قووت لەگەڵ یەکتر نوستن
تێر تێر یەکتریان لێسایەوە و هاتنە خوارەوە.
کاتێ هاتنە خوارەوە، لەوێ
یەکێکیان حەرفی ئەلیف ی لێ بەجێما
ئەوەی تریان حەرفی هێ.

دوو وشەکە لە خوارەوە دیتیان:
ئەو دوو حەرفەی لێیان بەجێ مابوو لەوێ
لەسەر گردەکە
پۆلێک حەرفی تریان لێ رووابوو
سەوز
تێک ئالاو
ببوونە درەختێک.

Head Hill

in the beginning was the Word

In the beginning there was a hill
a dry, bare hill
without any trees
without any shadows
that's why there was no life there.

Then a word appeared
at the base of the hill
then another word
together
they gazed at the naked hill
in the end they liked that hill—
they dared to climb it
to plant themselves.

The two words climbed the hill
they slept together naked
they licked each other head to toe, then came down.
When they came down,
one of them left behind the letter A
the other left behind the letter H.

From the foot of the hill, the two words saw:
the two letters they had left behind
on the hill
had grown a bunch of other letters
green
intertwined
they had become a tree.

پاشان ڕستەیەک پەیدا بوو
لە خوار گردەکە
ئنجا ڕستەیەکی تر
ئەوانیش حەزیان کرد بچنه سەر ئەو گرده خۆیان بڕوێنن.

ئنجا ڕستەیەکی تریش
لە کۆتاییدا چەندین حەرف و وشە و ڕستەی تریش
حەزیانکرد بچنه سەر ئەو گرده.

گرده مژه ئێستا
گردێکی جوان
سەوز سەوز
زۆر ئاوەدان.

Then a sentence appeared
at the base of the hill
then another sentence
they wanted to climb the hill, too, and plant themselves.

Then another sentence
finally, many other letters, words, and sentences
wanted to climb that hill.

Now Head Hill
is a beautiful hill
green-green
very prosperous.

Notes on Specific Poems

Withered Soul

Mahwi (1830s–1906) is one of the most iconic Classical Kurdish poets. After meeting the Ottoman Empire's Sultan Abdul Hamid II in 1883, he established a khanqah named in his honor in Slemani.

Being Seven

Piramerd (1867–1950), whose names means "Old Man" in Sorani, was a poet, writer, and journalist in Slemani. As editor of the newspaper *Zheen* he was a champion of Kurdish culture and values.

Tairawa / House Number 297

Tairawa is a neighborhood in Hewlêr whose name means "bird land" in Sorani.

The epigraph by Nali (1797–1869), another iconic Classical Kurdish poet who wrote primarily in Sorani, was translated by Shene Mohammed and Alana Marie Levinson-LaBrosse.

Longing

Ahriman is the name of the evil spirit in Zoroastrianism. He is responsible for human confusion and strife.

Nasir "Shaida" Mohammed

A chaixana is a traditional Kurdish teahouse, a center of community life for men, as well as a common venue for Kurdish writers and intellectuals to discuss and debate ideas.

You Should Have Waited, Sarwar!

Pirbal writes: "Sarwar Ahmad was 'my brotherliest brother, my friendlist brother, and my friend.' He was a storywriter and artist. In December of 1985, with his fiancée Beyan, he jumped into the Tigris River. Sarwar left only one collection of Arabic-language stories behind: *The Smoke from the Room*."

Biography

In the original, the title for this poem appears in English, written in the Kurdish orthography.

J

In Kurdish, this poem is titled with the letter ژ, which represents the voiced postalveolar fricative (/ʒ/ in the International Phonetic Alphabet). A common occurrence in English is represented by the S in the word "measure."

My Memories of Exile

Abdel Kader El-Janabi (b. 1944) is an Iraqi poet, translator, and journalist who settled in France after living in London and Vienna. In 1973 in Paris he founded the first surrealist Arabic review, *Le Désir Libertaire*, which was banned in the Arab world.

44 Definitions of Exile

Definition four, "Metamorphose," appears in English in the original.

Definition twenty-eight cites a line ("Oh how I love her.") from a song by Ali Merdan (1904–1981), a famous Kurdish singer born in Kirkuk, considered to have revolutionized the maqam. Mardan founded the Kurdish radio station in Baghdad in 1939.

Piramerd refers to Turkey as Rum, a then-common name, borrowing from the Persian phrase Takht-e Rum, "Throne of the Romans."

Arab Shamo (1897–1978) was a Yazidi writer considered by some to be the first Kurdish novelist.

Mehmet Sharif Pasha (1865–1951) was a prominent Kurdish nationalist and the second documented Kurd in Sweden, where he served as the Ottoman Empire's Ambassador. Often referred to as the "Father of the Kurdish Nation," his hand-drawn map of Kurdistan presented at the Paris Peace Conference in 1919–20 remains well known, featured in textbooks and used to decorate Kurdish homes.

Afifa Iskandar (1921–2012) was an Iraqi singer nicknamed the "Iraqi Blackbird." Born in Mosul to an Armenian father and Greek mother, she lived in Baghdad, where she also worked in the theater. She sang over 1,500 songs over the course of her career.

The italics in definition forty represent Pirbal's use of Arabic in the original.

Kharaman's Discussion of Khurshid's Letter in Response
Kharaman, the daughter of a Chinese emperor, and Khurshid, an Eastern prince, are the two primary characters in a Gorani love story attributed to eighteenth-century poet Almas Khan-e Kanoule'ei.

English Poetry Takhmis
The takhmis is a form of correspondence poetry popular in Classical Kurdish poetry, in which a poet responds to a couplet by another poet by appending three lines to it, producing cinquains until the original text is exhausted. The term is occasionally used to refer to cinquains that were not produced in this manner. In the current poem, Pirbal borrows poetic phrases from the English language, though without any clear attribution and not according to the traditional pattern of the takhmis.

In a note accompanying their translation of Hamdi Sahebqran (1878–1936) published in the May 2022 issue of *Poetry*, Alana Marie Levinson-LaBrosse and Shene Mohammed write about the takhmis:

> The form further fascinated us when we realized that Kurdish poets employed the form so much differently than any other linguistic or ethnic group around them. The takhmis descended from the musammat, a stanzic form that Islam's devout community used for exegesis, rendering the form, in most scholastic opinion, theoretically interesting and artistically dead. Kurdish poets working within a persecuted language use the form instead to celebrate and skewer each other's work, to reinvent the literature they inherit from the more dominant surrounding languages.

As ever, in this instance the poet engages in the takhmis tradition of reinvention and skewering with signature Pirbalian chaos.

Song of a Blue-headed, / White-handed Stranger
While seldom used in everyday speech, both "blue-headed" and "white-handed" are widely understood by Kurds, the former used to describe someone who brings ill-fate or is ill-fated, the latter to describe someone to whom things do not come easy.

Apprivoise-moi
The title appears in French. The slightly affected Italian of the poem's dialogue, written in Kurdish orthography, can be translated: "'There's a man in that house, but I don't know who it is.' / 'It's a foreigner searching for his childhood.'"

Bitter Nights inside the Dark Coffin of Reflecting on the Hexed Patriotisms of the Fratricidal War

References to fratricide in contemporary Kurdish literature typically refer to the Iraqi Kurdish Civil War, which took place from 1994 to 1997, splitting the region into two rival territories based on partisan lines.

Diyarbekir

This poem is in the Kurmanji variant of Kurdish. The underlying text, from Musa Anter's 1959 play *Birîna Reş* (Black Wound) can be found on p. 46 of Istanbul publishing house Avesta Yayınlan's third edition, published in 1999.

Refugee Number 33,333

Though few details of his life are known, Baba Tahir is believed to have been a poet and dervish from the Hamadan area, at the beginning of the first millennium.

The bald boy is a character in an ancient Kurdish legend. Seeking a cure for his mother's blindness, he encounters a demon on his journey. Killing it, he receives the cure.

Haji Qadir Koyi (1817-1897) was an iconic Classical Kurdish poet and proto-nationalist who championed the use of the Kurdish language.

Kurdistan Regional Government

Janiya, Ali, and Abdul Qehar are typical Arab names in Kurdistan.

Romantic Songs of Exile

Hawre and Hiwa are male names that mean "friend" or "comrade" and "hope," respectively.

Bachtyar Ali (b. 1966), here referred to by the endearing diminutive Bakha, which we have rendered "Ol' Bachtyar," is a contemporary Kurdish novelist and poet.

For Najmadeen Mala
Najmadeen Mala (1898–1962) was a Kurdish writer, journalist, and teacher, known for both the school and bookstore he founded in the city of Slemani.

For Hussein Huzni Mukryani
Hussein Huzni Mukryani (1893–1947) was a Kurdish historian and journalist from Mahabad. He established the first Kurdish printing house in Aleppo in 1915, relocating it to South Kurdistan in 1925.

For Zhdanov
Andrew Aleksandrovich Zhdanov (1986–1948) was a Soviet politician and cultural ideologist in the late 1940s. Widely considered to be Stalin's most likely successor, he preceded the leader in death.

In Kurdistan, "jackass" is a common way to refer to anyone considered to have betrayed the Kurds by helping the Ba'ath regime, which employed widespread civilian surveillance.

Anfal refers to the Anfal Campaign, a counterinsurgency operation directed against Kurdish civilians, carried out by Ba'athist Iraq in 1988, at the end of the Iran-Iraq War. Human Rights Watch has described Anfal as a genocide, estimating between 50,000–100,000 deaths.

For Sheikh Mahmud
Sheikh Mahmud Barzanji (1878–1956), a pioneering Kurdish nationalist, led a series of Kurdish uprisings against the British Mandate of Iraq and served as king of the short-lived Kingdom of Kurdistan in early 1920s Slemani.

For Ahmadi Mela

Ahmadi Mela (b. 1957), born in Shwan, Kirkuk, left Kurdistan in 1983, later receiving a master's degree in Linguistics and a PhD in Comparative Literature.

For Haşm Serac

Haşm Serac (b. 1954) is a Kurdish writer and critic from Hewlêr.

For Hêmin

Hêmin Mukriyānī (1921–1986) was a Kurdish poet, journalist, translator, and literary critic born near Mahabad.

For Qubadi Jali Zadeh

Qubadi Jali Zadeh (b. 1953) is a poet, attorney, and government official known for his frequent use of brief, haiku-like forms to express sensual imagery, often focused on women's breasts, the life of the peshmerga, and sometimes both. His transgressive 2019 poem "I Wish I Were a Dog," translated by Mohammed Fatih Mohammed and Shook, was published by Asymptote.

For Aziz Ghardi

Aziz Ghardi (1947–2022) was a Kurdish writer and translator from Hewlêr. A lifelong bachelor, he translated over one hundred books from Arabic, English, French, and Persian into Kurdish.

The Surah Al-Fatiha is the first surah of the Qu'ran, a component of many obligatory and voluntary prayers in Islam.

For Hamidi Qawami

Kamaran is a common male name meaning "happy" or "content."

Maghdid is a male name no longer in common use.

Saholaka Street, named for a famous ice factory once headquartered there, is the name of a popular street and entertainment district in downtown Slemani, where Kurdish men go to socialize over street food and tea.

NDP is an NGO in Kurdistan.

For Gharib Pshdari
Gharib Pshdari (b. 1941) is a poet and translator from Qaladize.

For My Son, Rodin, When He Turns 18
The lyrics "My homeland, my homeland," which appear in the original in Arabic, come from "My Homeland" ("موطني"), featuring lyrics written by Palestinian poet Ibrahum Tuqan (1905–1941) and music by Lebanese composer Mohammed Flayfel (1899–1986). An unofficial anthem of Palestinians and other colonized Arabs, it was adopted as Iraq's national anthem in 2004 on the order of Coalition Provisional Authority Administrator Paul Bremer.

In addition to being Islam's holy day, Friday is the first day of the weekend in Kurdistan, as in most of the Middle East.

Nancy Ajram (b. 1983) is a Lebanese pop singer and celebrity. Among the most followed Arabs on social media, Spotify has nicknamed her the "Queen of Arab Pop."

"Water of life" is common in mythology, as a source of immortality, and the phrase is also familiar in a religious context. Here Pirbal suggests Rodin's minders will replace the actual water necessary for human life with the imaginary or metaphorical.

Ayad Allawi (b. 1944) is an Iraqi politician who served on the Iraq Interm Governing Council established by US-led coalition authorities following the 2003 invasion of Iraq. He became the country's first head of government since

Saddam Hussein when the council dissolved on the first of June 2004, naming him Prime Minister of the Iraqi Interim Government. A former Ba'athist and founder of the Iraqi National Accord (commonly called Wifaq within Iraq) who has spent over thirty years in exile, he also served two terms as Vice President from 2014–18.

For Farhad Pirbal
Yaprax is a Kurdish delicacy similar to dolma.

Mahir was a singer from Rawandiz.

I Remember . . .
The epigraph by Sheikh Raza Talabani (1835–1910), one of the most transgressive of the Classical Kurdish poets, was translated by Shene Mohammed and Alana Marie Levinson-LaBrosse.

A tekye (commonly known as a tekke in Turkish or a khanqah in Persian) is a facility designed for Sufi gatherings and education. Typically featuring a large hall for performing religious rites and smaller classrooms for religious instructions. Tekyes often also have accommodations for traveling dervishes.

The Pearl Necklace (عقد الولو), directed by Youssef Maalouf (1914–1972), an Egyptian of Syrian origin, and Khaldoon Al-Maleh (1938–2016), one of the first Syrian directors, starred actor Fahd Ballan (1933–1997).

Qaimagh is a milk cream similar to clotted cream. It is popular across the region, particularly for breakfast.

Adnan Alkaissy (1939–2023), was an Iraqi professional wrestler and manager best known as Sheik Adnan Al-Kaissey, Billy White Wolf, a Native American character he began playing in Oklahoma, or General Adnan. Géant Ferré was an early ring name of André the Giant (1946–1993). A high school friend of Saddam Hussein, Alkaissy attended college in the United States on an American football scholarship—despite having never before played the game—at the University of Houston, before transferring and emerging as a wrestler at Oklahoma State University. In the early 1970s he produced several professional wrestling events in Iraq, under the auspices of Saddam Hussein, inviting and defeating the Scottish wrestler Ian Campbell and Canadian champion George Gordienko, as well as André the Giant, whose 1971 match to celebrate the fiftieth anniversary of the Iraqi Army attracted an estimated 300,000 packed in and around the Al-Sha'ab International Stadium, which had a standing capacity of 50,000. Alkaissy describes the events in fascinating detail in his autobiography *The Sheikh of Baghdad* (Triumph Books, 2005), written with Ross Bernstein, including Hussein's ringside pep talk, which terrified him for both wrestlers' safety:

> Be victorious, Adnan, we are all counting on you. Be victorious. This guy is big, but he is a pussy. I know you can beat him. If he hurts you in any way, he is going to get this. [He lifted up his coat to show me a solid gold pistol.] I will put a bullet in there in his fat head and send him back to France in a pine box. (pp. 86–87)

Al-Quwa Al-Jawiya is a Baghdad-based football club.

Hamze Kenas' name suggests his occupation as a street sweeper.

Lamiya Tawfiq (1937–1992) was a singer from Baghdad.

In the protest chant against decentralization, the phrase we translated "numbed by the nation" (پێمان تەزی), suggests the tingling sensation and numbness that follows a decisive blow.

The lyrics excerpted from popular Baghdadi performer Fadil Awad's popular 1968 song "No News" appear in the original in Arabic, but written in Kurdish orthography, hence our decision to use the Latinized Arabic. The song tells the story of a young man who returns from military service on the night of his lover's engagement to another man. Poet Zêdan Xelef's translates from the Arabic: "No news, / No bridal veil, / No sweet-and-sour candies, / No juices. / I hear your trays are filled with candles."

Abu Tubar, literally "The Hatchet Man," was the nickname given to Hatem Kazem Hathom (1932–1980), the perpetrator of a series of thefts and murders committed in Baghdad during the early years of Ba'ath Party rule. He was caught in 1974, admitted to his crimes on national television, and was sentenced to death by hanging at Abu Ghraib.

Reza Shah refers to Mohammad Reza Pahlavi (1919–1980), the last Shah of the Imperial State of Iran, overthrown in the Iranian Revolution in 1979.

Msto is the diminutive version of the name Mustafa.

Orosdi-Back was the first European-style department store in Baghdad, opened along with a Basra outlet in the wake of World War I. Founded by Adolf Orosdi, a Hungarian army officer who had sought refuge in the Ottoman Empire, the eventual international shopping behemoth opened its first clothing store in the Galata neighborhood of Constanople in 1855, eventually establishing itself as a multinational corporation in Paris and expanding across the Middle East, Europe, North Africa, and even Japan. At its height, it had an outlet in Hewlêr as well. In the common Kurdish pronunciation of the store name, the final syllable is pronounced /eg/, hence Pirbal's mother's name for it.

"She gave him a hug / Now his dad is a bug!" is our playful rendition of the phrase "Boys among girls / their fathers, beetles" (كوڕ له ناو كچان / باب قالۆنچان,), a child's rhyme suggesting that boys should not allow girls to play with them, a Kurdish version of the childhood concept of cooties.

The name Qembur means hunchback. The translators do not know why the cinema patrons shouted it.

Musa Anter (1920–1992) was a Kurdish writer, journalist, and intellectual assassinated by Turkish Jandarma İstihbarat ve Terörle Mücadele (Gendarmerie for Intelligence and Counter-Terrorism), the unofficial intelligence agency of the Turkish Gendarmerie General Command.

Media Hall is a large government auditorium in Hewlêr.

Kamal Fouad Jumblatt (1917–1977) was a Lebanese politician who founded the Progressive Socialist Party, who led the National Movement during the civil war against the Lebanese Front. Also a major ally of the Palestine Liberation Organization, he authored over forty books on a wide range of political, philosophical, and even literary topics, and was assassinated by unknown gunmen—suspected to be Ba'athists—in 1977.

Nechirvan Barzani (b. 1966) is a Kurdish politician currently serving as the second President of the Kurdistan Regional Government, having previously served as Prime Minister and Vice President.

Most Kurdish Jews were forced out of Iraqi Kurdistan in the late 1940s and early '50s, primarily relocating to the newly established state of Israel.

Waish is an expression of grief for oneself or another.

Newroz is the Kurdish New Year (commonly spelled "Nowruz" in the West, from the Persian spelling).

A pest was a type of early truck in the region, common in the 1940s and '50s, typically repurposed to carry passengers and recognizable by their wood-paneled sides.

During times when currency was scarce, merchants often gave customers matches in lieu of change.

Geli Ali Beg is a famous waterfall located about 130 km. north of Hewlêr.

Tholathy Adwa'a El Masrah (lit. "three lights of theater" in Arabic) was an Egyptian stand-up comedy trio famous for its humorous musical sketches. Their song "Sulalari" ("سولاري") was featured so frequently on Iraqi TV that the phrase became lexicalized to refer to something boring and repetitive.

The lyrics by Muhammed Ahmed Erbili (1933–2022), here translated into English, appear in Turkmen in the original.

A feqê is a student of Islamic and Quranic studies at a tekye, where he often boards, beginning as early as elementary school age.

Abdul Sattar Tahir Sharif (1933–2008) was a Kurdish academic active in politics from late 1950s through the '70s. He was assassinated in 2008, ten days after publishing an opinion column in the monthly *Livin*, criticizing Kurdish leaders for not pushing harder for the contested city of Kirkuk's integration into the Kurdistan Regional Government.

The Sorani lyrics to Sherzad Abdulrahman's song can be translated "Friend friend, soul friend . . . my eyes friend."

Giwi Mukryani was the publisher of Kurdistan Press. *Layla and Majnun* is an Arab story about the seventh-century Bedouin poets Qays ibn al-Mulawwah and his lover Layla bint Mahdi.

Rasul Gardi (1924–1994) was a musician from Hewlêr who recorded 615 songs during his lifetime, as well as compiling three books of louks and heyran.

The Kurdistan Toilers League refers to the Komala Ranjdaran, also known as the Revolutionary Organization of Toilers of Kurdistan (distinct from the Komala Party of Iranian Kurdistan, which remains active today), a Marxism-Leninism and Maoism-influenced party founded in 1969 and dissolved into the Patriotic Union of Kurdistan (PUK) in 1992.

Hezârfen Ahmed Çelebi (lit. 'Polymath Ahmed the Wise' in Ottoman Turkish; 1609-1640) was an Ottoman scientist, inventor, astronomer, physician, musician, and poet from Constantinople.

Samoon is a common Iraqi yeast bread cooked in a stone oven. Leavened with live-culture yogurt, it is often called "fish bread" because of its distinctive fishlike shape.

Mishko (1908–1989) was a popular singer of traditional Kurdish music, particularly beloved in Hewlêr.

Abd al-Karim Qasim (1914–1963) was an Iraqi army brigadier and nationalist who came to power when the Iraqi monarchy was overthrown in 1958. He remained in power as Prime Minister until his execution in the Ramadan Revolution of 1963. The neighborhood names Gomepîs and Julakan mean "dirty pond" and "the Jew's neighborhood," respectively. We've translated "We want to be free / from the headscarf's tyranny" to replicate the rhyme of the original slogan, "We want freedom / from the twist of the scarf and abaya!"

Uzair is a prophet mentioned in the Qu'ran, often identified with the biblical Ezra. After being dead for one hundred years, an angel miraculously revives him, along with his long-dead donkey.

The Kuran neighborhood takes its name from its many kilns.

Iskif means "thimble."

Fuad Ahmad (1933–2004) was a popular Kurdish singer from Hewlêr.

Hamu Al-Qadu was a large property owner and merchant in Mosul, known for his business connections to the United Kingdom and for his alleged avarice.

A Dinner on the Green Grass
Nouri al-Maliki (b. 1950) is secretary-general of the Islamic Dawa Party and was Iraq's first full-term post-war prime minister, appointed by the US Armed Forces Coalition, from 2006 to 2014, later serving on two occasions as Vice President.

Bashar al-Assad (b. 1965) has been president of Syria since 2000. He is also the commander in chief of the Syrian Armed Forces and the secretary-general of the Central Command of the Arab Socialist Ba'ath Party.

Abdullah Gül (b. 1950) was the eleventh president of Turkey, from 2007 to 2014.

Dondurma is a type of Turkish ice cream known for its hardness and resistance to melting.

The Postmodern Peshmerga
We have rendered the phrase دارا دوو داری دی, which means "Dara saw two trees," as "Dara digs a deep ditch," to replicate the alliteration of the Kurdish, as this phrase, a mnemonic device to teach the letter د (representing the voiced denti-alveolar plosive, roughly equivalent to the English-language sound typically represented by the letter D), comes from the first-grade textbook used in Iraqi Kurdistan.

Head Hill

گردەمژه, here translated "Head Hill" rather than the more direct "Suck Hill," refers to a hill near Goizha Mountain, a hill on the outskirts of Slemani, famous as a lovers' lane.

The epigraph is the first clause of John 1:1 from the Arabic Van Dyck translation of the Bible.

Acknowledgments

Thanks to the editors of the following publications, where some of these poems first appeared, sometimes in earlier versions and with earlier titles:

Caesura: "i," "Song a Blue-Headed, White-Fingered Stranger," "EXIL," "For My Son, Rodin," and "Romantic Songs While Abroad"

On The Seawall: "Tairawa / House Number 297," "Hotel Paradis," "My Home on My Shoulders," and "1993"

The Heart of a Stranger: An Anthology of Exile Literature (Pushkin Press, 2019): "Waste"

Thanks too to the editors of *Harriet* (Poetry Foundation), for publishing "A Poet Among Potato Eaters: An Introduction to Farhad Pirbal."

Thanks to Alana Marie Levinson-LaBrosse for allowing us to include her cotranslation with Pshtiwan of the poem "Waste," and to her and Shene Mohammed for allowing us to use their translations of several epigraphs excerpted from Classical Kurdish poems of the nineteenth century.

Thanks to Shene Mohammed for her diligent review of this translation, and for her clever solutions to some of this translation's most perplexing challenges. Thanks to Alana Marie Levinson-LaBrosse for her insight and patient collaboration, and for connecting us in Kurdistan, paving the way for this collaboration. Thanks to Zêdan Xelef for their help identifying and translating the Arabic-language lyrics in "I Remember . . . ," for their collaboration in translating the visual poem "Deyarbekir," including identifying the underlying text, and for their input on our translations of the other visual poems in this volume. Thanks to Massimiliano Lombardo for his help transcribing and translating Pirbal's Italian. Thanks to Stephen "Papal Bull" Di Trolio, for scanning a first edition of *Exil* at Princeton University Library. Thanks to Pablo Marín, for his graphic design expertise. Thanks to Jiyar Homer, cotranslator with Shook of Pirbal's poetry into Spanish, for his advice and insight. Thanks to Azhin Omer for her transcription of the Kurdish version of several of these poems. Thanks to Aza Yousif and Zhyar Aswad for their help contacting and arranging meetings with Farhad Pirbal. Thanks to Farhad Pirbal himself, for answering our many, many questions. May these translations bring you the same joy they bring us.

Biographical Information

Farhad Pirbal is a Kurdish writer, philosopher, singer, poet, painter, and critic. He was born in the city of Hewlêr in South Kurdistan in 1961. He studied Kurdish language and literature at Salahaddin University in Hewlêr, and was admitted to the Kurdish Writers Union in 1984, soon thereafter publishing his first book, a play titled *Farewell to My Country*. Upon completing his university studies, he was drafted into Saddam Hussein's army, and after twenty-three days as a soldier, he escaped to Iran. After eight months studying Persian language and literature, he acquired a visa to travel to Poland. With that visa, he reached Denmark, which granted him asylum. He stayed there for over a year, until he received a scholarship to study cinema in Poland. Soon thereafter he received a second scholarship, to study literature in France, where he matriculated at the Sorbonne. Upon earning his doctorate, he returned to Kurdistan and taught Kurdish literature at Salahaddin University. In 1994 he founded the Şerefxan Bedlîsî Cultural Center in Hewlêr. To date Pirbal has published over seventy books of writing and translations, including novels, collections of short stories and poetry, cultural criticism, history, and literary studies. In the last several years he has shown his paintings at major galleries in Kurdistan, performed as a singer of Classical Kurdish music, and hosted a television program about Kurdish culture. Pirbal's *The Potato Eaters*, translated by Jiyar Homer and Alana Marie Levinson-LaBrosse, is also available in English from Deep Vellum.

Pshtiwan Babakr is a filmmaker, curator, and translator. For three years, he served as the archivist for visual arts at Kashkul, the center for arts and culture at the American University of Iraq, Sulaimani, during which time he curated and co-curated exhibitions featuring artists such as Ismail Khayat, Goran Mohammed, and Hawre Khalid. Additionally, he directed and produced several documentaries, including *Red Land* and *Not for Sale,* which have received recognition at numerous film festivals worldwide. His translations have been featured in esteemed publications such as *World Literature Today, On the Seawall, Loch Raven Review,* and *Dispatches from the Poetry Wars.*

Shook is a poet whose most recent translations include Conceição Lima's *No Gods Live Here* and Jorge Carlos Fonseca's *Pigs in Delirium.* With Jiyar Homer, they translated Farhad Pirbal's selected poems into Spanish, as *Refugiado número 33 333* (Gato Negro Ediciones, 2022). Since living for two years in Slemani, they have cotranslated over a dozen Kurdish writers, including Xoşman Qado and Qubadi Jali Zadeh into English and Sheikh Raza Talabani and Bachtyar Ali into Spanish. Today they direct Kashkul Books, a multilingual publishing project based in South Kurdistan.

With fellow Pirbal translator Alana Marie Levinson-LaBrosse, Pshtiwan Babakr and Shook curated *Through the Smoke, Beging the Curtain,* a site-specific installation featuring the work of photographer Hawre Khalid at Slemani's Culture Factory in 2019. Babakr and Shook also collaborated on *A Barcode Scanner,* a prize-winning poetry film featuring the work of Zêdan Xelef.

9 781646 052714